PRAISE FOR *YOU, RECHARGED*

"In an age where constant exhaustion is the norm, Polly Campbell provides refreshing perspective and practical advice to live our best lives. *You, Recharged* is a must-read for anyone seeking to rediscover their most confident, energized self."

—Melody Wilding, LMSW, executive coach and author of *Trust Yourself*

"In *You, Recharged,* Polly Campbell writes about the idleness some (most) experience at middle age with a vulnerability that is relatable and honest. She has a way of allowing you to feel you're not alone in the lackluster lull that may hit in midlife when starting to wonder, *Is this all there is?* She also brilliantly illuminates the sources of power that are well within our reach to spark our hearts and recharge ourselves. This book is a recipe for you to access, reignite, and cultivate the spark to re-inspire your zest for life from the inside out. Polly shares practical, inspirational ideas to support a joyful and thriving life."

—Amy Schuber, energy healer specializing in releasing inherited ancestral trauma, intuitive strategist, and producer & host of *nspired Conversations Podcast with Amy Schuber*

"One of my deepest beliefs is that presence and energy are the biggest gifts we can give others. They're also our greatest gift to ourselves. Our vitality infuses life with delight. But what happens when we are flatlining, limp, uninspired, or weighed down? Here's what, we pick up this book! *You, Recharged* is the battery pack we can plug into whenever we feel drained of life force and no longer have that zip-a-dee-doo-dah that turns gray days to technicolor. Using curiosity, research, wit, and heart, Campbell shares her own processes and practices that recharge her life. Her fresh voice awakens us and she models the role that humor and compassion play along the way. This book is better than vitamins. It is a boost and thunderbolt. This book is your jumper cables. Plug in and GO!"

—Sherry Richert Belul, founder of Simply Celebrate and author of *Say It Now*

"Polly Campbell's *You, Recharged* makes rebooting your life easy, effective, and fun! If you've ever found yourself overwhelmed ten pages into a self-help book, *You, Recharged* is for you. Instead of the typical 180-degree turn lifestyle changes many books suggest, Polly offers a gentle, welcoming 'If I can do this, so can you' approach to revitalizing your life. She peppers her relatable experiences with research and provides simple, useful suggestions. The result is a workable plan for increased happiness and peace of mind. And who doesn't need more of that!"

—Nita Sweeney, award-winning wellness author of *Depression Hates a Moving Target*

"One thing I appreciate about author Polly Campbell is her realness. Readers learn from Polly's been-there, done-that, didn't-work personal stories as well as her accrued wisdom and experience. *You, Recharged* is about vitality and energy: what it is and how we can enhance our own. While her book is a treasure trove of information, insight, and practical applications, one of Polly's wise sentences, 'Energy builds from compassion,' struck a special chord in my heart and has become a personal mantra."

—Sue Patton Thoele, author of *The Courage to Be Yourself*, *The Mindful Woman*, and *Strength* among others

"*You, Recharged* is the all-natural prescription for our overwhelmed, fatigue-filled lives. In an inspirational and down-to-earth style, Polly Campbell shares real-life anecdotes and practical tools for regaining the zest and enthusiasm needed to overcome roadblocks and reach your goals. If you seek sustainable energy to power your dreams, this book can help you do that."

—Donald Altman, author of *Simply Mindful, The Mindfulness Toolbox*, and *101 Mindful Ways to Build Resilience*

"IF EVER there was a time that our population needed inspiration and ways to recharge, it's now. The candid and practical narrative Polly provides is a path forward. It's an invitation to rethink assumptions and choose a road to a deepened energy and revitalized hope for wellness. Feeling worn? Tired? Take Polly's hand..."

—Mary Anne em Radmacher, poet and author of *Live with Intention*

"If you're alive then you've probably experienced some low points in your life...times when you told yourself, 'somethings got to give.' You also probably struggled trying to figure out what to do about it. Struggle no more. With an abundant supply of ideas, this wonderful book will help you put your pain in the past. It's like a much-needed vacation that helps you recharge, reinvigorate and refresh your life."

—Allen Klein, author of *The Awe Factor: How a Little Bit of Wonder Can Make a Big Difference in Your Life*

YOU
RECHARGED

YOU
RECHARGED

How to Beat Fatigue (Mostly)

Amp Up Your Energy (Usually)

and Enjoy Life Again (Always)

POLLY CAMPBELL

CORAL GABLES

Published by Mango Publishing Group, a division of Mango Media Inc.

Cover, Layout & Design: Morgane Leoni
Cover Illustration: © Eigens / Adobe Stock

For permission requests, please contact the publisher at:

Mango Publishing Group
2850 S Douglas Road, 2nd Floor
Coral Gables, FL 33134 USA
info@mango.bz

For special orders, quantity sales, course adoptions and corporate sales, please email the publisher at sales@mango.bz. For trade and wholesale sales, please contact Ingram Publisher Services at: customer.service@ingramcontent.com or +1.800.509.4887.

You, Recharged: How to Beat Fatigue (Mostly), Amp Up Your Energy (Usually), and Enjoy Life Again (Always)

Library of Congress Cataloging-in-Publication number: 2020946295
ISBN: (p) 978-1-64250-488-0, (e) 978-1-64250-489-7
BISAC category code SEL021000, SELF-HELP / Motivational & Inspirational

Printed in the United States of America

CONTENTS

FOREWORD

What I love about Polly is her can-do attitude. No matter what life throws at her, she's always ready to get back up and keep moving forward. This same attitude is found in the pages of this book. *You, Recharged* takes us on an emotional and mental journey through the process of how Polly went from dreading life to recognizing faulty areas and choosing to do something about them!

Polly writes in such a fun and relatable way; reading her words makes me feel like I am sitting with her at my favorite coffee shop. I know exactly what she means when she talks about being frustrated with feeling stuck. Compared to any other book in its category, this book comes out on top twice over because Polly is super intentional with her relatable and easy-to-understand content. I have been a fan since discovering Polly's blog turned book *Imperfect Spirituality* and, once again, this wonderfully wise woman has just what I need, exactly when I need it, in *You, Recharged*.

With *Badass Affirmations*, I try to give little pick-me-ups and bursts of empowerment, but what Polly does in this book is amazing. She picks us up even when we are completely emptied out, borderline burned out, with nothing left in the tank. Let Polly take you by the hand and heart and get you back to how you are supposed to live: busy but not crazed, happy but not harried, and best of all, at peace with yourself. You can do it. You can recharge!

I love how Polly touches on all of the positives of adding things into our lives. In our world, so many gurus, speakers, and bloggers are always preaching and teaching about minimizing the material things and time-sucking activities in our lives. But Polly has a different approach: she focuses a lot on the benefits of purposefully and actively adding things that bring joy into your everyday life. Polly really goes in-depth at sharing so many easy-to-follow tips that will instantly recharge your thoughts and bring true happiness into your life.

You, Recharged is a book I will be purchasing for all my best girlfriends. I urge you to do the same and to try all of the tips and practices Polly writes out for you. With her words, your heart will surely be recharged to do just what is necessary for you to live a full and happy life!

—BECCA ANDERSON, author of *Every Day Thankful* and
Badass Affirmations

INTRODUCTION

Three years ago, I felt blah. Stuck. I weighed more than I wanted to be. My only pair of good jeans felt tight. I wasn't writing much. I lived with chronic pain and wasn't creating anything in person or on the page.

I felt sluggish. Tired all the time. Bored. Is this what a midlife crisis looks like?

The label didn't seem to fit. Life has ups and downs. The days felt dreary, but that's not a crisis, it's a mood.

We are drawn to the weight of words like crisis. The implied drama of it. So often a crisis refers to total devastation or a breakdown. I was neither devastated nor broken, but I wasn't thriving either. I was uncertain, frustrated, bored. Unsure of what to do next. It had been decades since I felt so stuck. And I didn't like the feeling.

A crisis can also mean a turning point for better or worse, an emotionally significant event, or a radical change of status in a person's life, as per the dictionary. Those definitions did seem to apply. A crisis is a decisive moment.

Yes. That's it. I was in a decisive moment. Would I stay stuck and sink deeper into my comfort zone, or opt to get up and launch into the next phase of my life?

No, this wasn't a crisis. It was an opportunity.

Midlife Malaise

The term "midlife crisis" was coined in the mid-1900s by Elliott Jaques in a paper he'd drafted for a meeting of the British Psycho-Analytical Society.

In that paper, Jaques talked about his study of great artists who also experienced a depressive period lasting several years between their mid-thirties and fifties. He speculated that others suffer this same midlife malaise, including an inability to enjoy life and "compulsive attempts to remain young."

After years of upward growth and expansion—college and marriage and kids and careers and new homes and new jobs—we hit a lull in the middle years that can knock us back, leave us feeling low, tired, and regretful, according to some psychologists.

Some people try to cope with the discomfort by making radical changes, filling the holes inside by reaching for things outside. Finding new partners, buying new cars, investing in plastic surgery. Anything to move off autopilot and feel like they are young and flying again.

I definitely wanted to recharge my life, to stop feeling so stuck and tired all the time. I was uncomfortable. Unsettled, but not in crisis. I was in transition and searching for a new place to land.

Life changes as we grow. My roles as a wife and mother had shifted because the people I wifed and mothered were growing and changing too. The one-two punch of arthritis and aging was messing with my body. My hair was getting gray, and I had a hard time seeing the football scores at the bottom of the flat screen without my glasses.

Life requires us to adapt and adjust, for sure. It isn't easy. Not always. But for the first time in years, I felt free to do it. Free to change my mind, make some new decisions, and go forward differently. I just didn't know what the heck that would look like. Or what I wanted next.

What now?

This book is about the *what now*. How I went from stuck and frustrated to recharged and revitalized and what I learned along the way.

You, Recharged isn't about being blissfully happy, it's about being fully alive. About living wholeheartedly. With a plan and simple practices, we can get unstuck, reclaim our energy, and step into this phase of our lives feeling capable, confident, empowered, and energized.

We can recharge. We can live with strength and vitality. No, we aren't in crisis.

This is our decisive moment.

PART I

The Problem

"Is this all there is?" I was sitting on the left side of the couch where I always sit, drinking the coffee that I always drink, wearing a hoodie that smelled like last night's pizza. I'd woken up ten minutes earlier. The morning still dark. Already, I was counting the minutes until bed. So tired. Burned-out. Bored.

"Is this it?"

The job. The kid. The house. The husband. The routine days. The same ol' work and chores. Is this what happens in midlife? We do it all. Hustle for years and then settle in, overtaken by boredom, fatigue, a kind of midlife malaise?

Enough. Something's got to change. I hated that it was me.

Yet there is hope in that too. When we get clear about the barriers and beliefs that separate us from the life we want to live, we can make a move. Do something. Get unstuck. Feel excited, enthusiastic. Energized.

Our problems are our responsibility—and that is the good news, because we can change them, and when we do, everything else changes.

First, we must understand the problem, get to the root of what's holding us back, keeping us dull and drained. The beliefs, behaviors, habits that are keeping us stuck. Then we can create a plan, supported by practices that will help us reenergize, reengage, recharge.

Not only is this process illuminating, but it's also invigorating and fun. It's about creating a wholehearted life. And if I, a middle-aged mother living with chronic disease can revitalize and recharge, so can you.

CHAPTER 1

BACKSTORY

Even if I hadn't searched up photos of hip x-rays on Google (and I had, of course, I had), it wasn't hard to interpret the image. The oblong edge of the hip joint a clear sign of the rheumatoid arthritis I'd had since the age of three.

It looked like fog rolling off the bay, settling into the boundaries of bones. Places that should have been white were gray and rough-edged, misshapen. A picture of the invisible grinding pain I'd felt for decades. A ghostly vapor chipping away at the hip joints, eroding bone now, limiting movement, sending flares of pain through my nerves.

"I think we can fix this," said the surgeon, pointing the metal tip of his pencil at the muddled intersection of bones.

"But you can see there is nothing left here. Haven't seen a hip this bad, well. Haven't seen a hip this bad."

Bone on bone. Both hips. Thanks to the disease that moved in when I was a kid. Now, in my late forties, a circuit of trouble running from toes to ankles, knees to hips, wrists to neck.

Docs talking double hip replacement. Then the knees. An ankle or two. Eventually, I might be able to walk the hundred feet from the parking lot to my daughter's soccer field without feeling like I'm on fire. Surgery. Surgery. Surgery is the answer, said the surgeon. Whenever I was ready.

I wasn't. Ready. So, I just nodded. Turtled my achy neck down between my shoulders.

"Okay. So, if I was going to do this," I said, "what should I do between now and then to make sure I recover?"

He tilted his head. Blinked.

"Maybe lose some weight."

On the way out of the office, a gray-haired woman pushing a walker passed *me*. Knitting needles and a tangle of yarn poking out the top of the purse strung over the rail. The corridor was approximately 7,323 feet long. I tipped against the elevator walls when I finally got there. Shifted my weight when one hip started burning. Then back again. Next to me, an older man, cheeks slack with wrinkles, leaned hard on his cane.

My mood matched the gray storm clouds cluttering the sky outside the gray concrete clinic building. Rain dappled the windshield as I swung out of the parking lot. Headed to meet my mom for lunch. Surgery. Surgery. Surgerysurgerysurgerysurgery.

Not ready to talk about it yet. Surgerysurgerysurgery. Will keep it to myself during lunch. Process. Won't say a thing.

For at least three minutes, as it turns out. Until after I order the French onion soup.

"Well, that surgeon, he's very good," Mom says. "All my friends have had their hips done by him."

That night, I sit in bed, a thriller cracked between my fingers. But I'm not thinking about that story. I'm thinking about my own. How it would change with a new hip. To walk without pain. To stand cooking in the kitchen or walk the dog on the cement sidewalks without discomfort. No longer would I stress about getting through airports. I could even vacuum again—not gonna mention that one to the husband. I understood that surgery would help improve my physical health.

But my head wasn't right. My heart wasn't in it, either. And I wasn't brave enough to go into major surgery and under anesthetic when I was in this, this mood. Feeling unfamiliar to myself and half-assed about life. Midlife malaise, maybe?

Clearly, my bad hips weren't the only things bothering me. I was stuck. Struggling. Feeling drab and dull. Most of all, I was missing a zest for life. That kind of core energy that percolates from within, creating a zest for life. This vitality is animating. It enlivens us, improves mood and health. It's essential to living a good life. And for a while there, my vitality had fizzled.

I needed to recharge.

But how was that going to happen? How was a chronically ill, middle-aged, overweight, sweatsuit-wearing wife, and mother of a teen (who was alternately loving and sweet and sucking the very life force out of her), going to recharge and revitalize when she didn't even feel like getting off the couch?

No clue. Not then. But I knew the answers wouldn't be found in the operating room.

It was clear that something had to change.

I hated that it was me.

CHAPTER 2

WHAT IS VITALITY?

I'm slumped against the left cushion on the blue couch guzzling coffee, trying to wake up after a night of too many slices of pepperoni pizza and drinks with more vodka than seltzer. My thighs and butt are fat with baby weight—the baby is now twelve. My favorite faded XL sleep shirt is snug across my belly, where it once hung loosely. And there is the pain. A siren sounding through my body, untouched by medication, keeping me awake at night. I'm counting the hours until bedtime. Fourteen to go.

I can see a spider's web of fine cracks inside the base of the white mug I'm holding. One of six gifted off the wedding registry more than fifteen years ago. I feel fragile, too. Like I'm cracking under the fatigue and frustration of middle-aged parenting and work, marriaging, and managing.

The wedding that brought me this mug also led to a committed marriage that now feels a little been-there-done-that familiar. The constant feed-the-cat-feed-the-kid-go-to-work-go-to-bed household routine of chores and meaningless work in a world that, some days, feels populated by people with no manners—a metronome of the mundane.

The Feeling at 47.2

Life can do this. A merry-go-round of transitions. Spinning from a jittery, active, excited, fired-up twenty-year-old to a confident, competent woman and writer in her thirties, to a dissatisfied, restless, stuck, anxious middle-aged woman adept at managing the remote and binge-watching true crime happened so fast, I barely noticed how I was changing. But the changes are significant for so many of us.

Research by Dartmouth professor David Blanchflower shows that after about the age of eighteen, our happiness levels take a dive, and we wind up feeling our most miserable at the age of 47.2 years. Roger that. He studied hundreds of thousands of people in 132 countries and found this "happiness curve" holds true in most countries.

Why? Well, according to Blanchflower, the bloom is off the rose early on after we recognize that surprise, surprise, we are not invulnerable, and we don't know everything. When we mature and recognize that we no longer want to be married to this person, or our dream career isn't all that dreamy, when we realize that we won't achieve our every dream or accomplish every goal, the disappointment dawns gradually.

But there is a moment when we realize that certain things just aren't going to happen. And our happiness takes a hit. Around this time, we start looking around and thinking everybody is getting along better than we are. Better jobs, better bodies, better spouses, polite kids who are never sticky. These people, well they have it all. They are even skinnier and fitter than we are. And for sure they have better hair and no dark bags under their eyes.

This is deflating, of course. And ridiculous. And, yes, I've done this. More than once. Maybe you have too, and this kind of social comparison and awareness leaves us feeling unfulfilled, dissatisfied, disappointed.

"I just feel like I'm in neutral," my husband told me one night. "Like I can't get going. Can't get any momentum."

So many of us share this feeling. My friends have mentioned a frustration that comes from not knowing what they want they want to do now that one career has run its course and kids are grown and gone. Clients have shared their own experiences of that weird middle ground between building a business and letting it go while there is still time to do something different. Memes on social media joke about it. This midlife malaise is a real thing, and then because we are the conscientious sort, we feel bad about feeling bad.

To get specific, we feel guilty that we are ungrateful, unhappy. Embarrassed. Frustrated. On paper, my life was good. Healthy kid. Comfortable house. Kind husband. Good friends. No riches, but enough. A career that I created—one many call a "dream job."

Jeez Louise. I'm embarrassed to even spell it out here. With so little to complain about, why was I so unhappy? Instead of feeling excited about what I was creating in my life, I was waking up to a husband snoring next to me and thinking "Whoa, how did I end up here?"

"Is this all there is?"

These thoughts and feelings drain our physical and emotional energy. We feel bored. Dull. Worn, fatigued, tired all the time. We begin to separate from ourselves a bit, become unsure about who we are, what we want to do next, what we care about now. After a lifetime of thinking we had this all figured out, we wake up empty. Not sure what we want. What we love. What we enjoy. What matters now. What makes for a meaningful life now.

I was 47.2 years old (but who's counting?), and I decided I didn't want to stay stuck in this low-energy life. Though Blanchflower's research does show that our happiness levels slowly increase into our fifties and beyond (it's possible to be as happy as you were at eighteen in your mid-sixties), I didn't want to wait. You guys, we just don't have the time. We need to go all in now. This is our decisive moment.

I decided to reclaim my zest for life, recharge right now, and rediscover my vitality—the quality that elevates everything.

That Get-Off-the-Couch Quality

In some ancient traditions, vitality is called chi, or qi—the Chinese word for breath. In India, the ancient Sanskrit word is prana—the power that flows in all living forms and performs vital functions. The early twentieth-century spiritual leader and Indian yogi Paramahansa Yogananda explained prana as the life force "possessing an inherent intelligence enabling it to carry out the life-sustaining processes."

Vitality, then, is energy. It is animating. It's a get-off-the-couch quality.

It's also contagious, say psychologists Martin Seligman and Christopher Peterson, who, in their research, define vitality as a kind of spirit "expressed not only in personal productivity and activity—such individuals often infectiously energize those with whom they come into contact."

This isn't a grasping, clutching, nervous kind of energy, but "vitality implies an infusion with positive energy," write Seligman and Peterson.

Rooted in the late fourteenth-century Latin word *vitalis*, meaning "belonging or pertaining to life," vitality is both a physical and a psychological state threaded throughout our lives. It is about how we feel physically and emotionally. It's the energy that emanates from us, and the energy we take in. It's deliberate doing, with a sense of purpose, and the wisdom to know it matters.

While our vitality is influenced by external factors like what we eat, how we sleep, and how people treat us, it is also an intrinsic quality, one that pulses or dims depending on our internal perspective and feelings.

And living with vitality, approaching life with this kind of energy and enthusiasm, also improves well-being. It makes us feel better, more connected and curious, happier, and more alive, and that generates even more energy. So vitality is also self-sustaining.

This is no small thing when it comes to living a happier and healthier life. Vitality is a reflection of our well-being, according to research led by Christina Frederick at the University of Rochester.

Seligman and Peterson say it contributes to our resilience and satisfaction in life, and cozies up next to optimism, gratitude, the capacity to love and be loved, and curiosity as the key character strengths most correlated with health, happiness, and well-being.

Vitality and Happiness

Positive emotion, physical health, purpose-driven activities, gratitude, connection—these things all factor into our vitality, and they also contribute to our happiness. It's not enough to be physically healthy or emotionally stable. It's not one thing. It's all of everything. Vitality is holistic. It is both created by vibrant spiritual, emotional, and physical life. And the source of it.

When we give attention to our whole being, we do get a boost of positive emotion and physical energy which eases stress and contributes to better health and well-being overall.

But, to do this, to recharge this essential core energy, we've got to consider our internal landscape as deeply and as mindfully as the external factors. There will always be external energy drains. To recharge, then, we need to laser our attention on the things that carry their own vibrant energy and use it to help build our core.

We can eat nourishing foods, strengthen our muscles, and cultivate optimism and resilience. We can improve our balance, make art, meditate, and energy is all around us—we must cultivate it and allow it in. We can do that by making time for the real and the magic by giving attention to what we can touch, as well as to the intangibles like the stunning fire of a sunset, sharing an inside joke with a bestie, or a quiet moment alone, knowing you did your best.

But here's the big question I had. If vitality is both a quality necessary to our health and well-being and one that requires it, what chance do I have? Can a chronically ill woman like me (who is feeling washed up at 47.2), live with this kind of Big Energy? Can you? Can we recharge at our core level and lead this kind of healthy and energized life?

Life smacks us around and zaps our energy. Our bodies get older. Sometimes we become more cynical. Tired. Knocked back by more change and transitions that chip away at our health and well-being. Are we to be left out then?

Does vitality belong only to the cool kids, like mountain climbers and marathoners, who seem to radiate good energy, good luck, good looks, and good health? Can we still be vibrant, energetic, strong, vital, even when we are oldish coffee drinkers?

Can we have this kind of energy with teenagers yelling at us to leave them alone, and after we botch a deal at work and scorch the microwave popcorn—again (seriously, is this the hardest thing to cook?). Can we have vitality if we even eat microwave popcorn in the first place? Can you have vitality when you are dressed in your pajamas by seven o'clock and snuggled into the couch to binge-watch your favorite true-crime show?

Yes. Absolutely. We can all recharge and love our lives again. Vitality is there for us too. And the best thing is, we get to define it for ourselves.

The Link

Research indicates that the things that harm our physical health and moods also dim our energy. Smoking, inactivity, overeating, lack of sleep, those things will knock us down. But pain, sickness, and age won't necessarily thwart our ability to recharge our vitality.

A study led by B.W. Pennix evaluated more than a thousand elderly women who were described as severely disabled. But researchers discovered something startling. Out of that group, 20 percent, 351 of these women, were defined as possessing "striking vitality" marked by a "high sense of personal mastery, being happy, and having low depressive symptomatology and anxiety." As a result of this emotional vitality, these women had a lower risk for new health problems and early death, according to the research.

Even people with chronic and debilitating pain can live with vitality, according to research. But our fear of pain, and the pressure of external influences—like doing things we aren't moved to do because others expect or demand it—diminish our vitality, making it harder to recharge.

We can overcome this. We can recharge when we ramp up our core energy with the habits and practices and attitudes that create more. Not only does this improve our health, it deepens our relationships, and improves our productivity, motivation, enthusiasm, and joy.

Vitality elevates everything. It doesn't mean you will be blissfully happy all the time, it doesn't mean a life without pain, but you'll feel less beat-up and more confident and capable when the tough stuff happens.

This is about living a more nuanced life. One of meaning and texture and joy. You won't feel so exhausted, counting the hours 'til bedtime from the moment you wake up, you'll be clear and present, able to immerse and engage with your favorite people and the best moments in your life in a wholehearted way. Vitality allows you to venture into the rough seas with more perspective and skill to recharge and weather the storm.

When you recharge this essential energy, you'll live fully. And that feels better than anything.

After all, we aren't here to hang out. Life is participatory, not passive. We are here to play, explore, love, feel, discover, learn, expand. We change everything we touch simply by the energy we bring. If you don't have it to drop on the potluck table, you'll find yourself where I was, on the last cushion of the couch, feeling depleted and hungry for something more.

When I realized that, I began to recharge my vitality. One baby step at a time. Building my core energy from the inside out, atom by atom, cell by cell, practice by practice. My way. I customized my own definition of vitality and drew out a plan that was two things—super easy and sustainable. Felt like a lot, considering I didn't even want to get up and get the coffee—but when I made the decision to recharge, everything changed.

Actually, that's not true. Not everything changed—just the things that mattered most.

CHAPTER 3

SUSTAINABLE ENERGY

Just thinking about how I could recharge my life sparked a little energy. I went from dull to curious. I started thinking about how much energy it takes to cultivate health, emotional intelligence, creativity, connection, and fun. I began considering where that energy comes from in the beginning and how I could get me some. It takes energy to make energy.

Think about one of your best days. A peak moment. What were you doing? Who were you with? I'm imagining you had to open the book, or make the reservation, or drive to the trail to make it happen. I'm imagining you gave out some energy to create the fun, or the art, or the relationship.

The best moments in my life—a warm Saturday with my parents in Autzen Stadium, a Fourth of July weekend at the beach with friends, happy-hour laughs with the core, eating olives in Italy, holding my baby for the first time, an important and insightful conversation with a friend, writing the first chapter of my first book—required an energy investment. I had to give some up to get some. But each of these things had a high rate of return. The energy I gave expanded and grew and fired me up, made me feel good, connected, healthy, vital, strong.

It takes emotional, physical, mental energy to have fun, to experience it, and then to process that experience, but then the fun energizes us. Vitality is self-sustaining, but it is not passive.

Yet, there was a Grand-Canyon-sized gap between how I was feeling and what I was doing, and what I wanted to be feeling and doing. How the heck was I going to close the gap when I didn't even want to walk across the street and get the mail? How was I going to recharge when I had no energy to give?

How can we live wholeheartedly when we are feeling low on heart?

My husband used to drive a red sports car. When we met, we'd climb into those seats, open the moonroof, drive the country roads listening to the Eagles, Neil Diamond, the music we remember our parents playing. Music that made September feel like summer. Years later though, I cussed that car every time I tried to fit the baby's car seat into the back. Now we drive a twenty-five-year-old station wagon with a dent in the driver's door (where I ran into a low post in the parking garage at my cousin's wedding), and a minivan. The van packs six teenage girls—if I don't go. I'm rarely invited. They prefer my husband to shuttle them around because he vibes with their preference for loud rock music.

But, on occasion, the Nasty Van—so named by our daughter because of its tan color and worn upholstery and doors that don't properly unlock—won't start. There is an issue with the circuits on the door panel and this one thread-like wire short-circuits the entire system, draining the battery. It's easy to jump. The cables are curled right behind the driver's seat. We connect them, and the van starts immediately. Then we drive it around for fifteen or twenty minutes so that the battery can recharge. It takes energy to build energy.

But I wasn't working like the van. Though I started my morning on the couch with a cup of coffee, within the hour I was taking the dog out, packing school lunches, making breakfast, responding to work emails. I worked full-time writing magazine articles, web content, marketing materials. Then there were soccer practices, orthodontist appointments, physical therapy appointments, vet appointments (dog's allergy shots), and a whole lot of other should-doing.

My days were full but instead of leaving me recharged, I'd crash into bed drained, burned-out.

A couple of years earlier, this same-ish routine had worked. It felt like a good pace, just the right level of busyness. I'd come off a demanding stretch at work, juggling several projects around my time parenting our young daughter. I was happy to settle into a predictable, less demanding routine. It felt comfortable and cozy, this plateau. But then it began to feel a little too comfortable. Uninteresting. Mind-numbing. I was complacent. Stagnant. Stuck. And I could literally feel the energy seeping out of me. And a sadness that I was unaccustomed to.

I also began to feel sicker. I'd spent all these years working to manage my chronic illness, and now it was lapping at me, like a rising tide against a shore wall. Pain and fatigue kept me from golfing—something I had loved—and walking the dog. I wasn't moving much at all.

And my baby? She was veering wildly into teenager-hood. And, according to her, she was fine with it. Had life all figured out. She needed something different now than the shoe-tying and hand-holding that I was used to.

I did offer her plenty of reminders. "I know, Mom," she'd say after every one. My marriage was comfortable, soft, like an old pair of jeans, but it felt a little faded, too. Even the job I loved had lost some luster. I was doing what I'd learned to do well, but not creating anything new.

Life had settled into a predictable pattern. It's like this. Energy ebbs and flows. There are times when we need to get quiet, take a breath, notice, appreciate, rest. That is a necessary part of recharging. It isn't an energy loss, but a slow simmer.

But I'd spent a little too much time simmering. My energy was flickering out.

Comfort turned to tedium turned to monotony. I felt overwhelmed by the smallest things. Coming up with dinner ideas tired me out. Sorting the mail seemed too troublesome. I was burning energy trying to figure out the grocery list and what colors to wash and what newsletter to send next, but I was doing nothing to kindle it.

Looking at the Lack

We all hit these places in life. Times when we need a jump start, a way to reignite that spark. But recharging isn't about getting busy—I was already busy, and that energy was spiraling out into the ether with no clear target. It's about deliberately doing and reclaiming to attract energy back into our lives.

To bring back the fun and the meaning, better health and well-being, love, and joy. This is where vitality is. This is what keeps it alive. This is how we recharge.

That's what I wanted. But first I needed to figure out what ignited my enthusiasm now. What energized and inspired me at this point in my life.

I got granular.

Dissected everything that wasn't working. Looked at what I was lacking. Made a list. It was a long one.

I was lacking energy, health, and strength. Comfort. My body was lit up by pain and stiffness. I was lacking enthusiasm and peace. I was missing a connection to my community—didn't feel like I was contributing. And my work wasn't feeling right, either. Wasn't interesting. I wasn't learning, creating, growing. I wasn't even making much money.

I felt ashamed. We live in a world with petrichor. Where frost plates fir needles like crystals. And on warm afternoons I can drink a caramel-colored beer with a squeeze of lime on the back deck with my friend of thirty years. There are dragonflies and sandpipers and ladybugs and good, hot, black coffee so strong it's nearly solid. Old, stretchy mom sweats, a cuddly dog, books. Mountain snow, roaring fires in stone hearths. And fountain pens that write smooth lines. Stars. Hearts that beat, without thought. All of this is within our realm. Yet, I'm sitting here too comfortable, complacent, stagnant. Lacking the energy to appreciate it.

Enough. Peeps, we just don't have the time for this. To play small. To settle into the thought that this is as good as it gets, that the fun is behind us. We are not built to sit idle, waiting for sleep, feeling dismayed that we are so tired and drained and bummed out.

Our spirits expand, our muscles strengthen, our brains grow, when we use them. When we activate. This is where health comes from, well-being, energy, joy.

We are energetic beings, wired to expand into life, to create it, and roll with it. That's why all this comfort-zoning stopped feeling good after a while. I'd recouped my energy, shifted with it, grown into it, and then I stopped. Settle in. Let it drain out.

Energy Drains

I'm a glass-half-full-refill-it-whenever-you-want kind of gal, so this drab feeling focused on what I was lacking felt a little off-balance. But when we can see the holes, we become clearer about how to fill them and the things we want most.

Often in my writing work and podcast, I talk with others who are thinking about these same kinds of things. I love those conversations. It's illuminating to share ideas and heartening to share a connection. But often, the very things people say they are missing—health, time, freedom, enough money, loving relationships—are things they already have. They just haven't noticed. In the process of striving for more, they lost sight of what they had already created. They just stopped noticing.

Energy grows, our mood elevates, when we fuel it with the things that matter to us. But we must notice what we have, celebrate what's there, or the energy dims.

For example, I was feeling dull at work. My creativity was lackluster. This worried me. Work had always been my go-to for an energy buzz. Now it felt confining.

I'd gotten good at the job over the years. Practiced. Fast. I'd been writing the same kinds of magazine articles for years. I knew just how to do them. That's what I'd worked for. But now that routine felt anything but creative. I wasn't experimenting or challenging myself to try different things or taking classes to learn new parts of the craft. I'd grown complacent.

But, helloooo—if we want something different, it's up to us to do it differently. It might feel scary or uncertain to make that first move, but when sitting around becomes a liability, when doing nothing is the energy drain, it is time to do something. We can't afford to ignore that pull. It's time to doodle, or write a meme, or pull the watercolors from the supply closet. Once you identify the drains, you'll see that the solutions, the things you need to do to refill that energy are often right there, built into your life. We have just become so used to seeing those things that we stop looking at them as sources of power.

My job—my life—still holds vast opportunities to create and grow and expand. So does yours. We are wired to grow; it's in our evolutionary makeup. Part of our survival. If we aren't seeing the possibilities of how we can do that, it's because we aren't looking close enough.

Other things are more obvious. I was physically tired all the time. I was also eating too much junk food and not sleeping enough. My body wasn't getting the nutrients and rest it needed for physical energy. That undermines our moods and confidence. It feels icky.

Yet, we live among the stars. We deserve to feel enchanted. When we don't, it's time to rise up. To recharge. When we lack vitality, it's time to back 'er up and take a clear look at what it is we are doing now, so we can figure out what would make us feel excited and engaged and energized again.

Once we know what we are missing, we recharge by filling up on all that good energy. By living close to the things that light us up, and when we do, everything comes alive, including us. I'm not overselling this.

Recharging our lives requires a holistic approach, to look at the things that support our mental and emotional health, our physical strength, agility, health, and our spiritual needs. To add in those that get those inner fires burning.

Cultivating Core Energy

This all starts from within. The core. Your very essence. That deep intangible place where our soul meets our solar plexus and creates this radiant life force. Vitality sits there. It also grows from there.

When you fill up on the things that inspire, excite, expand your entire being—your mind, body, spirit—you will recharge in the doing. Like driving the Nasty Van around to recharge a drained battery, you will fill up with energy by doing the things that fill you up, that add meaning, intrigue, instead of the things that drain you and offer little more than stress, boredom, burnout, fatigue.

Sustainable energy grows in incremental steps. Right now, look at the areas of your life where you'd like to feel a little more enthusiasm and interest. Consider the places where it feels as though energy is draining away. Are you eating too much junk food, watching too much TV, losing too much energy to work, or mindlessly scrolling through social media?

What would you like your days to feel like? What is one thing that might raise your energy level just a bit? Consider how you would feel if you did that thing. Fun? Relaxed? Interested?

Don't judge where you sit right now; just get curious. Look at what you're lacking, and then look for the possibilities that are there too. Find the things that are already present in your life, maybe something you've overlooked.

Choose one tiny thing to wonder about. Something that sparks your interest. Feel it in your body, daydream about it. Play with the idea of it. Trust that it's okay to feel connected and inspired and enchanted in your life again, even now.

Know that. Open to the idea of it. It's there for you if you choose.

Just start where you are.

CHAPTER 4

START WHERE YOU ARE

An inferno doesn't ignite all at once. It sparks, then smolders, before the flames appear.

But a spark only needs a little patience to get a good fire blazing.

The same is true for us. It's tough, when you aren't lit up by what's going on in your life, to think about what you want to create next. How you'll recharge and restore. We can smolder for a long time, there in that place of dissatisfaction and uncertainty. But that awareness is your spark. It's where curiosity begins, and we start thinking of something next.

Take it low and slow, give it time to catch. The tiniest baby step can move you from standing still to walking forward. All you need is to lean forward a little bit, then take a step to keep from falling, and soon enough you have tipped into a walk, and then, momentum, people. Momentum builds. One step swings into the next. A spark smolders into a fire.

The renowned monk Pema Chodron says, "Start where you are," and acknowledge and embrace the tough things in life, rather than denying. When we do this, we develop a certain intimacy with ourselves. An honesty.

Starting where I was meant I had to get to know myself differently because I had changed. I was no better or worse, just more layered. I wanted to live better in the now spaces between the big moments of life. The things I once cared about weren't priorities anymore. I wanted to feel more grounded. More thoughtful and measured. More aware and curious. This way, maybe I could invest my energy in the things that feel meaningful and interesting.

But how was I going to get there from here? From stuck, stagnant, and grouchy about it. I didn't know what to do next. I was so tired of working so hard. Despondent over the animosity, hostility, and sheer unkindness in the world. I didn't know how I could make a difference with all that. I didn't want to chase after goals, but moments.

I was anxious and irritable and impatient. Intense. Bossy. Sometimes I overtalk things. I definitely overthink them. But, rather than beating myself up, I decided to acknowledge. Accept all this. Recognize it. By becoming aware of all we are, we don't have to resist. This draws the energy back into our lives.

"Until we get to know ourselves, the imperfections and flaws, we cannot be in relationship with others," says Brad Reedy, family therapist and founder of Evoke Therapy.

Still, I smoldered in this place for a good long time, because I didn't know what to do next. Not exactly. What I did know was that I wanted to be free to change my mind, to learn as I went, to be a student again. Try new things. Experiment. And so I sat in this place of exploration and discovery and growth for a while. Then, I tipped forward just a bit. And I took a small step toward something better.

Okay Not to Know

If we are lucky in life, we compile years of experience just living. Just moving through time. And, as we accrue these days and hours, we learn some things. Get better at some of them. We become the "specialist" at work, or the supervisor, or leader, or mother, or elder. We buy into this idea of expertise. Thinking we have arrived, somewhere. Reached some level of knowledge or esteem.

It's easy to forget that we don't know it all. Not even close. It's a lot of pressure, in our forties, fifties, and beyond, to be in this place where we are expected to know certain things just because we've lived here awhile. But the most energetic lives are dynamic, so how can we ever know it all? This idea of the "expert" catches us up. It's scary to admit that what we know best is the uncertainty of it all. The knowledge we've accrued in the past worked then. But still there is much to learn about today.

My daughter used to ride the school bus to her elementary school. I'd walk her to the bus stop and then I'd go to work. One day, months into the school year, I decided to drive her to school for the first time. And, when I pulled into the parking lot, I was in the wrong lane. I didn't know it. I'd never dropped her off before.

I did notice several mothers glaring at me through the driver's-side window. But I was focused on doing my best drop-off because it's complicated. There is one drive-through lane, and a specially marked area—the only place—where kids can get out. And then there is a second lane on the outside for cars to pass through.

To my horror, or to be more accurate, the horror of others, I realized I was in the wrong lane *and* my kid hopped out at the wrong place.

The mother in the Suburban behind me made eye contact and shook her head. The parent volunteer stopped traffic in both lanes to walk over to my driver's side window for a leeetle conversation about my poor drop-off etiquette.

I had interrupted the flow of traffic for families everywhere. What I had done was *not okay*. And, if you are going to do drop-off again (after this, who would?), you'd better learn the rules.

I laughed later. But I also felt a little afraid and ashamed. Embarrassed. I mean, jeez Louise, what kind of mother can't do drop-off correctly? Me. Because I hadn't learned yet.

Listen, while it is very very wrong to not follow the proper drop-off rules, I'm okay not knowing other things. It's okay not to know, because then we are in that constant state of learning and growth. That's where the energy is.

We are bound to make mistakes, sure, but mistakes are movement. And when I was sitting there on the couch on those dark mornings, feeling stuck, not knowing what to do next, I didn't make a single mistake. I didn't make anything at all. And there is no vitality in sitting still and scared.

The energy is in the adaptation and change and exploration and discovery. It's not in the knowing. It's in learning. Not the mastery.

When we become good at not knowing, we are no longer stuck. We are free. Free to change our minds. Do different things. Experiment. Go all in. Become a beginner again even in our field of expertise, by trying innovative approaches, asking new questions, surrounding ourselves with art and nature and beauty and energetic thinkers and leaders. Growth is the fire we need to recharge.

I wanted to layer on my experiences, explore what I knew and what I didn't. I wanted to adopt new ideas and take a more try-this-and-see mentality. I'd played it safe for a while so I could be in the know. But that wasn't fun. It no longer felt good.

Age requires us to learn. We must learn to cope with loss. Adapt to change. Adjust to new roles as parents and professionals. It can dim our senses. Slow our responses. And some see midlife as a time to begin settling in.

It is not. It is a time of freedom. We don't have to care so much what others say. We are not compelled to establish our credibility, relevance. We are free to stand in our wisdom and free to define what matters now, to us. Then, we can live by that. Right now. We can start building the life we want, for now, moment by moment, even if it looks different from the life we've been living.

I first logged into the Internet in 1995 through a dial-up connection. It was the fastest thing around. Packed with energy. Now, of course, that old modem wouldn't have enough bandwidth to download the volume of emoji-filled emails I get, but it was the star at the time. The Internet grew off those early systems. Changed and upgraded.

The way to recharge isn't to compare yourself to your younger days. Or to do only what you've always done. It is to recognize how those moments—the bad and the good—were amazing.

To see how they infuse you now. Can energize you now. Now is where the energy is. We are dynamic, expansive, creative people, able to slip into the energy stream of life whenever we want. We can change our minds. To get up. Do it how we want. Breathe it all in.

Breathe It In

A couple of weeks ago, my daughter had her braces tightened and green bands (?!) woven in among the wires pulling at her teeth. Her mouth started to ache, and a headache throbbed. And she wanted to come home, because she hurt, but mostly because she wanted to skip science. But she stayed at school. I refused to pick her up, because, I am *that* mom, and it was time for science class, and she was regularly looking for ways to skip science. She wasn't happy that she had to stay. But, by the end of the day, she felt proud. Said she'd done her best. It wasn't all that good on that day, she told me, but she gave what she had.

She took more notes than usual, she said, because she was having a hard time paying attention and didn't want to forget the lesson. She stopped complaining and tried to focus on the good things about the class; her friend Elle is in it. And she got through it.

Then, something interesting happened—after the class, she actually felt better. Sure, her mouth still hurt, but she was happy with herself. Proud. Confident. More capable than she was before. She felt like she'd done the tough stuff and gotten through it. She felt strong.

Sometimes the best we can do isn't all that good, but that is not wasted time. Consistent effort over time is the difference-maker.

It's showing up every day that matters. It's giving our best—in that moment—and being gentle with ourselves.

In his book *Taoist Secrets of Love*, Mantak Chia writes "Taoist masters spent a lot of time observing the flow of this 'chi,' which they recognized as the breath of the Universe that moves through everything. Chi is the glue between our body, mind, and spirit, the link between our perception of the inner and outer worlds."

Some days, I'll have more physical strength and energy than others. I may feel a bit negative or stressed on Thursdays, when I'm late for a deadline, or I may feel strong and relaxed after I have a powerful workout or good connection with a friend. But, on all of those days, I can have vitality. I can do the things that recharge my energy, rather than let it drain to empty. Even if my best effort and energy look different from day to day—it is always enough.

Be your chi. Vitality is sustaining. It is the air around you and within you. The physical link that keeps us tethered to the universe. It doesn't come and go with good and bad days. It is always. And that means it's always smoldering within us.

This is no small thing. Our fire is not out. Start where you are. Just take a deep breath and bring it back to life.

CHAPTER 5

STUCK NOT DEPRESSED

One thing I needed to sort through when I was feeling fatigued and stuck was this: Was I stuck and burned-out? Or was I depressed? It's an important distinction.

Burnout can often lead to depression. Transitions and life changes and menopause and chronic illness and pain can too.

The good news is, both burnout and depression are treatable, but how you approach the symptoms and conditions will differ depending on what's going on. What is going on for you? Right now?

This is all about self-awareness and deliberate living, remember? It's not about shame. Illness, depression, burnout—these are not failings, they are conditions, like broken legs, and lactose intolerance, and migraines. Whatever you are feeling, make note of it. Reach out to your doctor—which is what I did in one of my very first practices to recharge—to find out where you are. Then, you can work with that.

Would exercise help? More sleep? A gratitude practice or antidepressant recommended by your doctor? Good. Want to work with a naturopath? Great. Need a mental health day off? Take one. Can acupuncture give you a boost? Try it. Think counseling would help? Do it. I *love* counseling. Whatever you need— whatever the treatment is to get you to a better-feeling baseline so you can put the plans and practices in place to recharge your mind, body, and spirit—do those things.

Over the years, I've found great benefit from therapy, medication, regular medical support, acupuncture, exercise, happy hour with my besties, golf, staycations and quiet time, meditation, rest, petting the dog. Lots of ways to do it, but all start with assessing where you are. Work with experienced doctors and counselors to help you identify what might help. Give your biological being, your mind, your emotional self, and your spiritual side the support they need, so you can fill up on the good stuff in life that will help you recharge.

What Depression Looks Like

During those gray mornings on the couch, when I was feeling lethargic *and* restless, I searched "what is fatigue a symptom of?" on my smartphone.

It was a bonehead move. I got about a quadrazillion results. Most were super scary, linking fatigue to diabetes, cancer, depression, pregnancy (?!), menopause, anemia, prostate problems (uh-huh), alcoholism, giardia, lack of exercise, lack of sleep—duh—thyroid disorder, arthritis (been there done that), anorexia, ADHD, eating too much dairy, not getting enough vitamin D—anything you can imagine.

Often, the fatigue we feel is linked to some not-so-good habits. Poor nutrition, lack of activity, not enough sleep, chronic illness. Ding, ding, ding. I checked all of those boxes.

Fatigue and an overall lack of energy can also signal depression, according to the American Psychological Association. Other symptoms of depression include changes in weight and sleep patterns, inability to concentrate, feelings of excessive guilt or worthlessness, thoughts of suicide, and other negative thoughts and feelings.

Many people with depression also experience apathy and just don't feel like doing anything. They no longer enjoy the things they once did. Depression can make it impossible for us to get out of bed in the morning.

If you are experiencing any of these symptoms for more than a few days, call your doctor. Talk it over. Depression is the most common mental illness. It can spring up at various times in our lives, and is often influenced by menopause and other biological and environmental changes. It is highly treatable through medication and therapy.

I did talk to my doc. And, after considering many variables, I realized I wasn't clinically depressed, though I do have sad and depressing thoughts on occasion. Sometimes they linger for a few days, but generally, I go to bed optimistic, curious, and open to what life will bring the next day. I was interested in doing *something*, I just didn't know what. That's where I was stuck.

My days and decades had been filled with parenting and working and striving in a very focused, hands-on way, and now, with a more developed career and an older child, the way I approached those roles needed to shift. My energy didn't have to be so fractured. I could be more focused now.

During the decades of busyness, I'd also either dropped the things that kept me engaged and grounded, or, at best, practiced them inconsistently. My once-daily meditation practice was now sporadic. I worked out, for about five minutes a month. And I was no longer developing new work. I was tired of myself. Tired of the routine. Tired.

But the distinction was clear—I did want to get out of bed in the morning. To drink coffee. I just didn't know what I wanted to do after that.

CHAPTER 6
IKIGAI FOR NOW

In Okinawa, Japan, they have a word for the intangible thing that makes you want to hop out of bed in the morning. No, it's not coffee. It's ikigai.

Ikigai is a map for living, says Tim Tamashiro, the author of *How to Ikigai: Lessons for Finding Happiness and Living Your Life's Purpose.* It's not one thing, but the intersection that occurs when we do something we love, that we are also good at, and that is something the world needs. Ideally, you'll also make a living by doing this thing. Ideally. Not always.

Loosely translated, ikigai is our purpose. The reason we get up in the morning. The meaning in all the madness. But this is where it gets tricky because we immediately panic or feel frustrated and whiney when we don't know what ours is.

Perhaps the purposeful, I've-got-it-all-figured-out zeal you once paraded through life with has abandoned you now that you are older than twenty-six, and have kids and a house payment. Maybe it's lost in the must-have job you took after the divorce. Or the work you've spent decades doing no longer spins your wheels. Perhaps your schedule requires long days at the office, doing the job of two people (budget cuts), while also getting a contractor in to fix the roof, dropping the kid off at soccer, so by the end, you no longer know what you know. And no longer care. Life changes in unexpected ways; we can lose sight of what drives us from deep down.

I thought my purpose was clear. At seven, I decided to be a writer. I was nerdy that way. What I didn't know then, as a second-grader, was that I had it all wrong. Writing had been an essential part of my life. Part of my health, expression, growth, job. The way I process the world. Create.

But I felt anything but creative during those early mornings sitting on the couch, smelling of pizza. The writing felt drab. The work uninteresting. And I freaked out a little. Felt like I'd come untethered from a bungee cord over a rocky canyon. If I wasn't a writer, what was my purpose? What was I supposed to do?

Research shows that people who define themselves as having a purposeful life experience greater meaning in life and more robust well-being. They have lower levels of cortisol, the "stress hormone" that often leads to greater inflammation and disease.

Purposeful living is linked to a decreased risk of early death in those over fifty, according to 2019 research led by the University of Michigan. Researchers analyzed data collected over twenty-five years from nearly seven thousand people fifty and older, and found those that lacked a connection to purpose were twice as likely to die as those who had it. And having a clear sense of purpose adds meaning and energy to our lives.

Sounds nice. We are more vital when we are living our ikigai.

But what if we haven't discovered ours yet? And there's still laundry to fold and taxes to do? We must deal with difficult people and make sales quotas, manage a budget and a household. Where is the ikigai in cleaning the fridge or sitting in the drawn-out conference call?

It's there. Within you.

Ikigai from the Inside

Our purpose, or ikigai, is an expression of ourselves, not our job.

It exists within us and outside of our jobs and roles and labels. I'd thought my purpose was to write. What I know now is that writing is one way I express my purpose—not the whole enchilada.

My job—writing—is the way I learn. It helps me to understand my life and translate ideas and emotions and experiences in a way that I can better understand, a way that might entertain or inform or inspire others. Our ikigai, however, is always bigger than our jobs. Mine, I discovered, is to inspire and encourage others with my words. Writing is just one tool I use to do it.

Tamashiro says it like this: "Our purpose is not our job, it's our work."

Writing helps me hit the ikigai intersect. When I write what I love, the stuff I'm also good at (because I practice so dang much), I can maybe provide a little something of what the world needs—hope, compassion, humor, helpful information—and make enough to pay the bills.

See the distinction? I thought writing was *it*. When I was burned-out on writing, I felt unmoored. I was doing my job, but not the work. I was expending huge amounts of energy doing things that paid the bills but straying from my ikigai.

My stuckness was a warning shot. A clear indication that I had strayed from my ikigai because living from purpose isn't exhausting, it's enlivening. Literally, life-giving.

The Layers of Ikigai

Ikigai starts as a nebulous thing. A cumulus cloud of layers. One feeling, stacked on a hunch, on top of an idea that creates this resonance where things just feel right when we are doing it. Life feels a little easier, more interesting. More meaningful. Ikigai often feels like flow.

We feel good, so we keep going. We practice. Try out our ikigai. Get creative. And customize it to fit who we are and our lives now. We become better at this thing—and more confident. We share it because we can't not, the world needs it. Ikigai is not separate from us anyhow, so it shows up when we show up.

If we are deliberate and open, ikigai appears in how we friend and work and parent and create. In how we love. In how we live. We find ourselves looking for ways to ikigai-ize—to live on purpose. Because it feels good. Right. Authentic.

Sometimes others take notice too. We become known as the person who lightens the mood, the one who is first to offer a helping hand. Someone who has a great artistic flair, or the one who has the wisdom to share. We become the one who nurtures with homemade bread or innovative ideas, or a resilient attitude, or leadership ability. The one who encourages. Or brings the fun. This is the work, then, Tamashiro says.

Tamashiro's ikigai, he says, is "to delight." That's his work. Not his job. His job is myriad. He's a musician, radio broadcaster, speaker, author, and dad. But in each of his roles, in every role, he has moments and methods to delight others. If a job is lost, such as the events that were canceled during the pandemic,

Tamashiro could still find ways to delight. Ikigai doesn't end when our paying gigs do.

This revelation recharged me creatively and professionally because I didn't have to push so hard to find market solutions or right answers to live on purpose. I could just play. Experiment. And use my words to do it.

I started a podcast. Began developing another book—two jobs that are also my work. And it prompted me to take on a slew of new creative projects that haven't yielded a dime or a dollar but have boosted my energy. That momentum has carried over into my jobs, so I could be more productive even while tackling the household chores or the writing work that pays the bills. I'm excited about writing again. Recharged.

Ikigai is not a job, it's a life. I can encourage my daughter, visit my friends, build a new website, and cook spaghetti, and still live my ikigai. That's where the meaning comes in. It's not what we do, but what we bring to what we do, that is ikigai. When we are on purpose, we are more satisfied, more open, better able to roll with the ups and downs of life, and that momentum helps us to expand into ikigai in other unexpected ways.

Discover the Intersect

Sometimes, though, it's the thing that buries you, the challenge that makes you question everything, that illuminates your ikigai.

That's how it felt to school psychologist Tricia Thompson when her elementary school daughter was diagnosed with epilepsy and her teenage son was struggling with difficult learning challenges. She had another preschool-age daughter home at the time too.

From the moment Trish got out of bed in the morning, it felt like life was piling on. She was pulled between a demanding job she loved, that also provided essential income, and the significant challenges facing her own family.

She was frayed, stressed, unhappy, scared.

But Trish began experimenting, later leaving her district job to become an independent network marketing sales associate for a health product company. This gave her the time flexibility she needed to care for her kids. As part of her trainings, she was reading about leadership and success strategies, connecting with other women, and delivering products and support that she believed would truly enhance their lives.

Supporting students and families had been Thompson's work all along. Only the job had changed. Trish has gone on to form Learning Without Limits, a consulting business where she works directly with families to support students with learning challenges. She works from home, so she's there when her kids need her. Her oldest daughter has outgrown epilepsy and made a full recovery. Her son will soon finish high school, something that at times felt unlikely. And Thompson continues to help others through her work and her jobs.

If you are feeling worn, dumped on, stuck, overwhelmed, unhappy, hollowed out by the end of the day, you could be out of alignment with your ikigai. Pay attention to those worn ragged feelings; they will steer you away from what isn't working.

And notice those moments when what you are doing feels right. When you feel like you are in alignment, even when the job itself is hard. Then look at the patterns that occur when you feel in that flow.

Consider these:

1. What would you love to be doing that you aren't doing now?

2. What do you feel you are really good at?

3. What is fun for you?

4. If you had unlimited energy, time, and money, what job would you do? Why?

5. What did you love doing as a kid?

6. What do you miss?

7. What patterns can you identify in your life when you've felt energized?

I love long slow dinners and deep conversations with friends. I'm fascinated by psychology and how we can use our brains to create the outcomes we want. I love books. So much. I've always loved them because I like big ideas and new thoughts and learning and creativity and stories. I want to bring that feeling to others. To leave them excited and encouraged. And that's the same thing I want my keynotes to do. And my podcasts. Sometimes that's my job. Always, it's my ikigai.

Now, it's your turn. Go back and look at the things you loved doing, or the times you felt most satisfied in your life. What were you doing? Take a look at the part of your job you love the most—what skills or talents does that require? Often, our purpose remains fairly constant—if we like teaching, we often enjoy teaching others throughout our lives—but the way we do that looks different.

A teacher may work with his students, then volunteer for a literacy organization teaching English as a second language, then spend time with his grandkids, teaching them how to mow the lawn. The work, the ikigai, is the teaching.

An attorney who works for equal rights and social justice causes, representing clients from marginalized or underrepresented populations and educating the public about the injustices, might also write novels on those topics. Creating another avenue to educate others about the issues.

Thompson sells health and wellness products that she believes enhance the lives of those who use them, and she is a learning specialist who helps enhance the lives of students with learning challenges and the families who love those students.

Our Ikigai is present always; our expression of it—whether it's to delight, or nourish with food, or inspire, or teach, or end social injustice—is vast and dynamic. That's where the energy comes from.

That energy is both the impetus and the outcome of ikigai. The exploration and the end. And the discovery process itself is exhilarating because you get to play and experiment and try things and release others until you settle into the thing that seems to fit.

Today, think about what you will do and consider these questions:

· Does it involve something you love?

· Can you tweak it, add to it, create something new, or adapt the thing you do until it aligns better?

- Can you find a way to draw it into your other roles and responsibilities?

- Are you good at it? Can you improve?

- Is it something you can be paid for?

Using your imagination, look for the patterns in your life. What did you do when you felt the most engaged and energized? What is it about that activity, hobby, chore, job, connection that fires you up? What are some of the moments in your life when you felt most energized and enthusiastic? What were you doing?

Visualize how aspects of those things could thread through your life now, with all your well-earned wisdom and moxie. Love to work out? Maybe you'd like to teach exercise classes. Enjoy reading? Post a review online; perhaps you are an evolving book reviewer. Let your imagination go. Explore.

Then, play, try new things, see what sticks. See what feels meaningful, interesting, delightful, resonant. Follow that energy and you'll identify your ikigai, and energy and interest will ripple and begin to recharge.

CHAPTER 7
STORM SURGES

People say the hardest thing about raising a child is the sleepless nights. They will tell you about the tantrums and the messes, the spit-up, and stickiness. They complain about the adolescent angst, school drama, costs of college. These things are true. Valid. But these things were like a stage one tropical storm compared to the annual student Science Fair that blew up every spring.

The Science Fair felt like a Category 5 howling from the bedroom down the hallway into the living room, where the table was covered with clippings and markers and paste a week before the day of the display.

Nobody told me it was coming. I didn't predict it. And when I heard my daughter talking about it, in the fall of her sixth-grade year, it all seemed easy enough. Students pick a topic. They research and develop it through the semesters—loads of time. Then, theoretically, they pull it together into some kind of public exhibit that usually looks like a three-paneled-poster board loaded with facts and images. We have one child. How bad could it be? I was literally panting with enthusiasm to see what our little scholar would come up with.

"Ooh, the Science Fair, you can do something really fun and interesting," I told Sweet P early in that first year. She looked at me and blinked.

Then I was all like, "Whatever you come up with will be so cool."

Months later, the day before she was scheduled to present, the board was still blank, except for a faint paw print near the smudged line of the H. H for hurricane. Scraps of paper left from cutouts littered the floor. Markers without caps and clear tape. Sweet P was running between the printer and the board, like a woman about to miss her plane. On her way down the hall, I threw a glue stick from the craft closet at her. "Just paste the sucker down and let's be done with it," I yelled.

But I did learn something. And no, it wasn't to Beware of the Science Fair. Well, it wasn't only that.

What I learned was that it's the storm surge—the wall of water and wind that follows the hurricane—that is often the most devastating part of the storm.

The winds on the right band of the eye (relative to the direction it's going) can reach more than 100 m.p.h. But it's the surge, trailing after the storm, that does the most damage. All the steaming, churning energy in the eye of the storm is released into the air and water. The winds push the water, and waves ride on the top of the surge, rushing onto the wind-battered beaches, filling the streams, and streets, rivers and roads, with water and wind carried with such a force that the cars and buildings even miles inland can be submerged.

If the hurricane lags, churning slowly near the shore, the surge can change the entire landscape. The surge doesn't energize the hurricane. The energy of the hurricane fuels the surge that follows behind.

When we make a move, no matter how big, we create our own surge. The energy we bring churns and builds, creating a spiraling momentum that persists long after our initial effort blows through.

The smallest movement from our stuck place of familiar routines and complacent comfort creates energy. That gets everything churning and turning. Hard to get started, sure (was for me), but once you do, even the slightest movement creates a ripple of energy that can surge into an incredible flow.

Often, we want the reward without the effort. It's daunting to get up off the couch, or have a difficult discussion with your partner, or tell your boss you want to do something different. To take a step into a new place, away from the terrain we've already mapped. But one step changes the energy of everything. One gust of wind can knock down barriers to everything else.

You step into your life with one action, and the surge that follows behind that carries you. You get up and lace up your walking shoes. Once there, it's a little easier to go for a walk. Where you meet up with a neighbor, who mentions a new volunteer committee, and could you help? Of course, you want to say no, but you are flooded by this energy surge, so you say yes, and you walk back to your front porch knowing something has changed. You moved a little bit. You feel a little better.

And the energy surges, and pretty soon you get caught up in it. You start thinking of new ideas and people who can help and it continues to shift and churn and move into different parts and different things and it's a dynamic, fluid thing—but the surge will push you and the momentum will carry you. Breaking the inertia. Tipping you forward into the next step. Into your vitality.

PART II

The Plan

I needed a structure—supported by some skills and concepts—to help me recharge and stay that way. To help me create a sustainable lifestyle that would support me through the ups and downs. It's not enough for us to know where we want to go; we need some training wheels to help us balance as we find our way there. To give us something to fall back on, and to help us find our way back to vitality when we get tired and mad and snarky and veer wildly off course.

To recharge would require a move from my comfort zone. So the plan I came up with had to help me stay the course, even when I felt uncertain or out of sorts. It needed to not only help ignite my energy, but also direct it.

We don't have to white-knuckle it through life—it isn't about being disciplined, it's about being deliberate, agile, involved. With this plan, the benefit is in the day-to-day doing, not the outcome. This is where I started and what I came up with to create a lifestyle, to elevate everything. I think it can help you build some powerful habits, too.

CHAPTER 8
TAKING INVENTORY

I met him in September, though we'd been talking for a month online when online dating was still scandalous. He drove up in a shimmery red sports car. It was new.

In those days, I could still bend low enough to get in those tight bucket seats. Felt like sitting in the space shuttle. And when we were inside, with the moonroof open and the stereo on, it felt like summer. We rolled around in the light breeze and soft light talking for hours in that car, rocking out with the windows down, holding hands, listening to the Eagles, thinking about possibilities. Everything about those few weeks in 1999 felt free.

He loved that car. I loved being in it. We drove it to our wedding. But when we sold it a few years later, I had no problem watching it back out of the driveway. We'd outgrown it. It wasn't easy to fit a baby seat in the back.

That car seat—which is like carrying an enormous picnic basket with a boulder inside—would catch up on the edge when I pulled the lever to tip the front seat forward. Even then it was hard to climb into the narrow back to buckle the baby in. We bought a station wagon. Wasn't glamorous, but even now, it's a tool that better supports our lives today. It allows us to take care of the things we value.

A friend once told me that everything has an expiration date. Even relationships. Because life is fluid and dynamic and we are all growing and shifting. We grow out of things. And it's hard to imagine when you're in love with the car or the memory or the moment or the man. It's hard to imagine when the shoes are new, or the computer is fast and the keyboard clean. But then our business expands, our lives change, and the technology, the cars, and computers, houses, offices—the infrastructure of our lives— no longer fits. It needs to change too. The scaffolding that holds the pieces in place. It isn't a sad thing. It's a growing thing. We make space for new possibilities.

So we set up a garage sale or donate the shirts we no longer wear. If we are fortunate, we buy the new shoes we need, when the others are worn. We give away the shirts that now feel tight along the ribs. We quit our jobs and go out on our own. Donate the couches and lamps and baby toys. Trash the broken cords and coffee makers and the Barbies with missing heads. We recycle our used paper and used cell phones and used black bean cans.

We let go. Recycle. Replace. Release our stuff to make room for things that work better.

Why, then, do we hold on to our old ideas? Our thirty-year-old beliefs about what our family should look like, or the work we ought to be doing, or how we should look when we are fifty?

We cling to the ideas and values and beliefs we grew up with, and by midlife, they fit about as well as that senior class T-shirt you found in your drawer last weekend. Actually, the one I found in my husband's drawer last weekend.

"It still fits," he said, pressed into that cotton casing.

"Yeah, well, I think it's a leeetle tight. You've, erm, bulked up since high school."

"Well, that's true," he said, flexing. Then he put it back in his drawer.

/ / /

We do this in every part of our lives. We stay in a relationship or a job or routine that doesn't quite fit us because it's worn soft. It's comfortable and familiar. We know what it requires. What we must do. Or we spend time doing something we don't care much about, because we believe we ought to, or it's polite or expected. And it may be, but that doesn't mean we need to be the ones doing it. It doesn't mean that old T-shirt looks good just because you can squeeze into it.

Forcing anything takes time and resources, energy. When we feel drained by our days, feeling like we are circling around the midlife crisis cliché, it's not because anything is wrong with those routines or jobs or relationships or T-shirts—it's just that we've outgrown them. They don't fit the life we want to lead now. We've changed and outgrown our existing values, needs, and desires. This isn't a crisis. This is growth. But we've got to allow it. Make room.

Sometimes this hits us from behind. We feel stuck—like those mornings I awoke so tired even after a long sleep. We feel out of sorts and uncomfortable and we don't like it. So, we think, a new car, a new relationship, a new house—a fresh start—now, that would make us feel better.

Of course, it doesn't. The problem isn't the thing. It isn't the work or even the husband. At least that's not where the problems start. It starts with us. With the frustration, we feel when we don't spend the energy we have on the things we care most about.

Knowing What Matters Now

The first part of any plan to recharge is to figure out, then, what it is we do want. What do we value now? What do we need to feel excited and interested in our lives again?

This is an act of discovery. Not always an easy or comfortable one. Even if the routine we've been living is a bit blah, it's familiar. We know just what to do. It's served us for years. Decades, even. But that's the problem. It no longer applies. The values and beliefs that have supported us for years are outdated. We've outgrown them.

In the last ten years, I've raised a toddler, written several books, and shifted from a full-time career to at-home parenting and back again.

Now, the toddler is a teen who can feed herself, help with the chores, and no longer wants to play with Barbies or build forts. Thank goodness! I have different energy too. It takes more to stay active. Heck, it takes more to stay awake. I stress less about most things. More about others. My parents are older. My marriage is seasoned. So the values and principles that guided me when I was newly married and had a baby are outdated. They no longer fit. They need an overhaul and an update.

For years, one of my top values centered around work and career development. I wanted to build a writing business and make enough money from it to support myself. I was passionate about it. I was twenty-two years old. Single. Self-reliant. Fast forward to a billion years later, and this has fallen way down the list. I still value my career and love my work, still need to make a paycheck. But what matters more to me now is the creative expression and positive contribution. Doing meaningful work.

I was comfortable in my job, but not creative, and that sapped my energy.

So I got to work trying to figure out how to do the work that inspires me (and hopefully others) and still provide the income my family needs.

Match It Up

But how do we do that? How do we rediscover and reestablish the values that guide our life when we can't even sort through all the shows that are streaming to decide what to binge-watch next?

Start by paying attention to the fatigue in your life. What leaves you feeling tired or overwhelmed? What do you have to gear up to do because it feels so hard? The fatigue you feel means something. Stop and contemplate the things you are giving your energy to. Where is it going? Then, consider what you would rather be doing or feeling. What feels more interesting, or meaningful? What would you rather be doing with your time? What do you feel curious about?

Pull out a sheet of paper.

In the left margin, write out your top values. You can define them however you want. Drop a few words down to indicate what they represent to you. Stick to about five-ish.

Mine include family and friends, physical and mental wellness (which for me means strength and fitness to do the things I want to do), creativity (exploration), freedom (some say "how I use my time"), integrity, and positive contribution.

Then, on the right side of the page, make a list of the things you do on a regular day. I make breakfast for my daughter. I connect with sources and people for my podcast, I stretch or get some movement. I write. I read. Sometimes I meditate. Sit down with the family for dinner. Do the dishes. And so on.

Now draw a line—like you would in an elementary-school worksheet—matching up the left-side values to the right-side activities that support that value.

For example, in my left column, I've written health, family, and creative expression, among other things. In the column on the right, I have physical movement, sitting at a desk writing, making the bed, helping my daughter with school, family dinner, and other details. I have lines going from the family value across to family dinner, from health to physical movement, from creative expression to writing. But I realized in doing this, that I didn't do much to support my creative value. This visual helped me change that and inspired me to create the podcast.

If you have values that don't match up to any action or activity, there's a gap. You may want to change what you are doing—or adapt the value. Either way, you want to create a match.

Check in with yourself. What do you care about? How are you spending your time? Do those things support each other? Our lives are an expression of those values, so take a look at how you are expressing yours. How do they appear in your life now? Are you expressing them through your work and relationships, activities, hobbies, the organizations you support? Are you spending time and energy on the things that fit your priorities? If not, your energy is escaping.

Slip into the activities, jobs, classes, organizations, friendships that align. This gets our energy going. Gives you a little feeling of confidence, as you step into your life. Create your own mantra or mission statement to help you move closer to what you care most about. Pick specific activities, events, ideas to develop that align with your values. This is where our core energy lies. Living close to the things that inspire us, that we value, is a key part of any plan to recharge. Once you recognize what you value, you can invest more in doing those things, and life begins to hum.

CHAPTER 9

MAKE UP YOUR MIND

Recharging our minds, bodies, spirits—reanimating our lives—requires us to get off the couch and get back out *there,* into a mosh pit of moments that are captivating and curious. Exhilarating. To create art and meaning. To connect more deeply with friends. To be a conscientious business leader, or school volunteer, or a more available parent or spouse.

But, if you're like me, thinking about all this, developing a plan to recharge in my mind is easier than getting up off the couch and doing it. Easier than moving out of my comfort zone into a new world of people and possibility.

When we get down to the specific actions, self-doubt creeps in. Excuses emerge. We say stuff like, "I'd write the book if I had time." "I'm too old to learn a new language, it's easier when we are young." "My body is too old and out of shape to start hiking or surfing or traveling now." Or my personal favorite, "I can't afford it."

We are tempted to nestle back down between the couch cushions, talking about how tired we are. But we are not those people, my friends. We are not. We want vitality. We want to feel alive and make the world a better place. We are putting a plan in place to recharge, and now it's time to back up our ideas with an attitude.

Not like the eye-rolling, big-sighing attitude I get from the teen whenever I sing along to her songs, but the attitude you can adopt to help you learn, improve, grow, and get better at anything you work at. It's called a growth mindset, and it is kick-ass. Aside from that, it will also propel you and help you persist even when you feel unsure and insecure.

Growth mindset is a concept introduced by Stanford psychologist Carol Dweck, that is all about believing you can. Research indicates that people who assume a growth mindset believe that they can improve and grow, so they are more likely to study, practice, and access the people and resources they need to create that growth. This is essential when we are moving from the zone of comfort into something new and different, something unfamiliar.

Think about it. If you want to learn to play the piano, you may not know where to put your hands at first, or how to play the B chord, but with the GM attitude, you are open. You aren't worried about making mistakes (okay, maybe a little, but you'll get over it) because you believe you can improve. With this in mind, you are more willing to experiment.

Historically, those of us born in the Stone Age were taught that certain people were bestowed with great intelligence and ability and the rest of us were just out of luck. The belief was that our brains and abilities were "fixed." Not born smart? Too bad. Two left feet? Bummer.

Now we know this isn't true. Science shows our brains are elastic, expanding and developing throughout our lifetimes with exposure to new tasks and things. We can improve. We can learn new things. Effort matters, and attitude matters.

When I started golfing again after a decade away, I had no illusions that I'd ever be on tour, shooting low scores. But I believed that, the more I golfed, the better I'd get. I learned from my bad shots and my good ones. Tried different techniques, got tips from others, and adjusted. When I failed, by hitting atrocious shots, I adjusted and tried again. And again. That is part of the fun. With a growth mindset, failure isn't a problem, it's a possibility. It's an outcome that gives you useful information. Not a character flaw. So you don't feel threatened by imperfection.

I'm still not a good golfer. But I am a better one, now. I keep trying, I keep learning. I believe I'll get better, one stroke at a time. Getting involved in the game again has helped me recharge, but it's the growth mindset that has made it feel like fun instead of a failure.

Before you decide to get up off the couch to recharge, choose to make a growth mindset a part of every plan, everything you do.

This will take some of the worry and discomfort away by making it okay to show up unpolished, imperfect. A growth mindset is an engine behind our actions, whereas the pursuit of perfection short-circuits our vitality.

Choose the GM

For me, a growth mindset is also an antidote for burnout. In the past, my MO was this: Get the Big Idea. Go All In. Push Hard. Work Hard. Stay up all night overthinking, overdoing. Get frustrated when things don't move as fast as I want. When the work doesn't go well. When I'm rejected. Feel tired and burned-out within weeks.

Growth mindset takes the pressure off. We are rewarded for consistent effort over time—not only for outcomes. We have room to fail, to be imperfect, because that is where growth comes from.

Authenticity. Personality. And even thinking about this makes me want to exhale, because when we have a plan that includes this mindset, we are free to dabble and play and adapt and change our minds.

There is nothing to get right, only things to learn, and this is so freeing. When I adopted this attitude, it became okay for me to write stories even if I'd never sell them. It became part of my personal and professional development to start doodling and playing ukulele and playing golf again. It freed me up to do some new things just to see what would happen. Just for my own fun and growth. And, not only did that approach lead to this book, but it also improved my health and my marriage, and opened up my creative expression and the income I make from it.

Used to be, I didn't make anything unless I could sell it. I got good at it. I also became bored, stifled, and the articles reflected that. My work started sounding like everyone else's in a world where editors want "fresh." A growth mindset springs the lock on complacency.

With this attitude in my back pocket, I launched a podcast. I took a brief class to learn about it, wrote a few episodes, and dropped *Polly Campbell, Simply Said* a month later. Long before it was polished and perfect. I felt nervous, insecure, excited, and exhilarated all at once. But I knew if I followed my usual approach and waited until everything was "perfect," I'd never get it done.

And I didn't want to stay stuck in that place anymore. We don't get stronger by sitting on the sidelines. We build our strength when we move. In the years since, the pod has grown astronomically, and so have I.

As you create your own Recharge Plan, hang your beliefs and ideas on this attitude of growth. Use it as a guide to move you into the next moment, the next phase of your life. It will take the pressure off, open you up to more interesting things, more of the fun and joy, and help you revise some of the beliefs that might be holding you back.

CHAPTER 10

ROUGH DRAFTS AND REVISIONS

I had my life story all written before I graduated from college. I'd move to New York City, work as a magazine writer, catch cabs and meet for drinks and gallery showings after. Didn't plan to marry. Didn't want children. Now, thirty years later, I can hear my teen rapping in her bedroom at the end of the hall, in a home located in an Oregon suburb. And I drive a minivan. I'm that woman. And I like it.

That first story, I realized, was a rough draft. I revised it quickly when I met the guy with the red sports car who didn't want to live in New York City. The internet came and the story changed again, because I could write for magazines while sitting in my sweats and every once in a while glancing out the window at the towering fir trees shimmying in the wind. I haven't taken a cab since the last time I went to New York, as a tourist on Broadway. My minivan is parked in the driveway.

You could read my story many different ways. The weight of a story, the power of it—whether it's our own, the ones we read in books, or those we overhear while waiting in line—is a result of the meaning we ascribe to it. So the story of my changing plans could be a tale of opportunities lost. You could see it as a love story—girl gives up her dream to stay with a cute guy, which is kinda Hallmarky. But those plot lines never occurred to me. Here's what did.

I changed my mind. And when I did, I also changed my story. Instead of missed opportunities, this was a story of choice. The choices to allow love into my life, stay close to my parents, and remain in the mountains of green. That story seemed to fit me better, at that time, than the one I'd outlined in my head years before. This revised story became part of my narrative identity.

We all have one, according to researcher Dan McAdams. Our sense of self becomes part of the stories we tell about ourselves. They become part of our identity. It's always been through story that we learn about the world, process our experiences and challenges, shape our values, and create meaning in our lives.

But it's the narrative that we tell and how we tell it, the tone and words and emotions we use, that gives the story resonance, creates meaning and purpose, and influences our behavior and beliefs about the world. Tell a bad-luck story and you're likely to get it. But it's yours to write and rewrite. You can revise it throughout your life, and when you do, your life changes.

Our life story—researchers call it life narrative—helps us process our present experience, but it also integrates the past with the future we imagine. In our stories, the past, future, and present are all part of the same plotline.

In one study, researchers evaluated a group of freshman college students who were struggling and at risk for dropping out. Most wanted to quit, some were depressed. Freshman students are often at high risk for drop-out, addiction, and suicide due to the pressures and changes associated with college.

Researcher Timothy Wilson asked these high-risk students to write about their experiences. Before doing so, some of the

Chapter 10: Rough Drafts and Revisions

students were told stories of how others struggled in college and then went on to great success. Other study participants were told nothing.

Those who weren't given any additional information continued to struggle. Yet those who heard the stories of others revised their own. They reinterpreted their own experience. In the end, the students in this group were much more likely to stay in school and succeed.

Instead of failure and depression, they considered a new story of adversity and triumph. And that's the one they began living.

When our story includes our ability to manage adversity and prevail, we are empowered and likely to create those circumstances. But what if the story of our past is about hardship and trauma and adversity and bad luck? Then we identify with that, and the story we tell of our past becomes part of our present and future narrative

Think about it. What if I told my New York story this way: I was forced to sacrifice my dream because the man I fell in love with wouldn't live in New York? Feels like a sad narrative of self-sacrifice that could lead to resentment and regret. Instead, my story was of strength, empowerment, choice, love. Happy endings. That has guided me to create a powerful storyline ever since.

When we change the meaning of our past story, we change the stories that we tell now and next. But here's the thing, we can also revise the stories we are telling right now to assign a different meaning to our memory and rev up our future.

Your Story to Tell

We all hear these profound tales of resilience. Children who tell incredible stories of struggle. Trauma, hardship, poverty. But these are really stories of strength. Stories about how struggle made them strong and determined not to recreate the trouble in their own lives. Yet, their brother, standing right alongside, raised in nearly identical circumstances, continues to struggle with depression and alcoholism, dissatisfaction and anger. How we experience the world depends on the story we tell.

I've witnessed the power of telling an empowering story in my own experience. I was a young child, three years old, when I was diagnosed with juvenile rheumatoid arthritis. There weren't a lot of treatment options then, and I was a tough case. I didn't grow into remission. I walked stiffly, had swollen, knotted joints, and pain that made it hard to sleep or, some days, to do much at all.

But my story about this was not one of hardship. I had chores to do. Read books. I rode bikes and recorded cassettes with music from the radio, crammed behind the coats in the hall closet. A friend tucked back in there with me too. I sold sno-cones. Went camping. My parents, my doctors, my teachers, all encouraged me to try different things and do what I could. We didn't talk much about what I was missing—instead, we revised the story and adapted the circumstances so I could find a way to be involved.

My story changed over the years, as I grew into my awareness. But my family and I always told a triumphant narrative. I didn't realize until later that others were telling other stories.

One night at a play, I ran into my former babysitter. She had taught me how to tie my shoes when I lived on Columbia Street. She was

Chapter 10: Rough Drafts and Revisions

pretty and cool and fun and had a boyfriend, who had a car, then. And she was just as kind and friendly all those years later, when we met as adults in the theater.

"I'm so glad you are okay," she said, giving me a hug, "I used to hear you moaning while you slept. I knew it was hard for you and I always felt so bad."

Perhaps it was hard. But that isn't the story I'm telling.

Revising Your Story

If you've ever gathered with family, or even a group of longtime friends, for Thanksgiving or a long meal, you know how it can go off the rails. And that usually starts with a story. Because even though we've shared many of the same moments together, we experience them differently. We assign different meanings. While my babysitter told a sad, compassionate story, my childhood tales were happy and active. But beware of plot twists that can change the meaning of everything if we let them. In those moments, make sure you are the one telling your story. Then you can be the Rocky of the plotline.

When I hit the midlife-malaise phase, I became tired of the story I was telling, the one about challenge and fatigue and illness and frustration and boredom. There was a gap between the story I was living and the one I imagined myself in. The one filled with adventure and intrigue and fun, strength, and good hair.

During these drab early mornings curled on the couch, unable to sleep but not fully awake either, I began to consider which direction my story would go next. How did I want the next chapter to read? And the one after that?

It was time for a narrative revise. After all, all we are doing here, until the story is permanently written on the day of our death, is a rough draft. We can revise the story we tell and rewrite the meaning to the one we've been living, and when we do we become the triumphant hero.

But instead of focusing on where I was and what wasn't working, what was missing, I started thinking about what I had, how much I had gained. I summarized the story of my life and realized all the good and bad had prepared me for this moment. Primed me for everything to come. This time, this age, isn't an end of our power, it's a culmination of it. This is a coming together of the confidence, the wisdom, and the experience that we've been developing and learning and cultivating our entire lives for this moment right now. This isn't the end of our interesting and productive time, it's simply the prep period for the next one. The one we start writing right now.

You get to tell your stories too. They belong to you. Create the ones you'd like to read because they are even more fun, more engaging, more interesting to live.

What are the stories—good or bad—that have shaped your life until now? What tales have you given meaning to? Now ask yourself this: Do those stories help you? Or hurt you?

Your identity and the way you engage in the world is determined by the meaning you give, the story you live. So, as we develop our plan to reengage with our world and live a robust life, creating new stories and new meaning, evaluate the ones you've been living with. The ones you are already telling.

Ask yourself these questions:

Is this story serving you?

Do you like telling this story?

No? Okay. Rework it a bit. Make sure that you aren't just replaying the bad bits or focused only on the losses or traumas. Also, take a look at how your main character—you—has overcome adversity. Some change has occurred, because you are a living breathing human. And you've survived it, changed, and grown. Make sure your story isn't solely focused on where you started, but also on how far you've come. Note it. Look at what you've gained.

You can think about the hard things that have shaped your experience. The adversities you've encountered.

Then, make a note of how you've faced them. What worked? What did you do well, what did you fail at? It's okay, we've all had those ups and downs.

What did you learn from them? Thinking back now, were there any benefits to the challenges? Have you grown because of them? Have they taught you things that have helped you in your life? Can they serve you going forward?

No wrong answers here—it's your story—but what I've seen in mine is that the challenges and adversities I've faced have helped me to become more compassionate, determined, resilient. Things don't blow me up like they used to. I don't stress out much anymore. I believe in my resilience. I'm capable of getting through anything. May not like it, but it will not take me out. That feels powerful even when I'm scared or unsettled. In the end, I think the next chapter of my story will be about how I recharged and reinvented my life, living well and healthy well into my later years. At least that's my story.

Now, what is yours?

Editing in the Good Stuff

Telling the stories that support us and the things we want to create in our lives is like a hit of caffeine, a jolt that reminds us of the path we are on even when times are hard—because that's part of the journey too, right, we have to have a story about how we had to run to school barefooted despite the thorns and rocks on the path, because then we get to tell the story of overcoming, and that is the ultimate display of our strength and tenacity and determination and brilliance and yes, you are all that.

So those challenging plot twists in your stories—like the freshman having a hard time in college, or the experts who suggested my body would be crippled, or the professor who told us writers would need to sacrifice income for their art—those stories can motivate us forward. To bust out of the limitations. As long as we don't believe every story that is told. The next time you think you are stuck in a bad-news story, do a simple edit.

Storyline. Want to lose weight, but you have this story playing about your family and big bones and how hard it is for you to lose weight?

Rewrite. It hasn't been hard to drop the weight by eating more nutritious meals. People are starting to notice something looks different about me. I feel great.

Chapter 10: Rough Drafts and Revisions

Storyline. I've always had bad luck. Now, with layoffs coming down at work, I'm sure I'll lose my job. Everything always goes wrong.

Rewrite. I've faced some big challenges, but always found my way through. I'm resilient. So, whatever happens, I'm capable of dealing with it. I'll be okay.

Take a look at some of the low-energy areas in your life, where the cobwebs drape, the places in your life that you feel are lacking in vitality. Just one. Maybe you aren't doing your ideal job, or you aren't as fit as you'd like to be, and you want to revitalize that thing. What is the story you've been telling yourself around that? What is the story you could be telling?

The stories of our past don't have to be the stories of our lives. Our last chapter does not need to be our next. We can rewrite, revise, and recharge by making the stories we tell next be about exploration, exuberance, love, connection, and fun. We can tell stories about good health and well-being. Of our triumph when we learned to live full-on by tapping into our core essence and our greatest energy.

And in the process, we make our own history.

CHAPTER 11
ADDITION +
SUBTRACTION

Life is a mix of taking in and letting go. We had to let go of that sports car, the one we had when we first married. It was in pristine condition, but it no longer fit our lifestyle. We wanted to make room for a baby. So we sold the sportscar, bought a station wagon.

Sometimes we hang on to things, ideas, beliefs too long. I'm looking at you, pink, crewneck college sweatshirt. We become attached to the idea of them. The memory. We cling to what once worked, even if it doesn't fit us any longer. Sure, those college days were fun. But I haven't worn pink in thirty years.

We do this with our values, of course. And we do this with our habits and behaviors. We hold on to what we've always done, what we know to do. This not the way to elevate our energy.

But the solution isn't to start tossing everything out. Changing every idea or philosophy. That just leaves us feeling clingy and needy. Nope, the way to recharge is to add more of the good stuff in. More creative expression. More growth. More inspiration. More gratitude. More fun. More healthy habits. More positive mindsets. More of the qualities and beliefs and behaviors that help us reboot our energy. From now on, our Recharge Plan is going to be about adding in the powerful stuff.

This shift in thinking has worked better for me. When I think in terms of cutting back and cutting out, stopping bad habits and behaviors, I get all nervous. A little needy and grasping. Think about it—if someone told you that today was the last day you could ever eat chocolate, what would you do? Probably power down as many Hershey bars as you could find. We tend to hold white-knuckle tight to the things we fear losing. Hanging on even if they don't serve us.

To get out of this pattern, a sustainable plan must include filling up, expanding, adding to our lives—not deducting from them.

Thinking like this changed things for me immediately. In the past, when I was trying to break bad habits, I cut back. To save more money, I stopped spending. To lose weight, I eliminated the foods I liked. Disciplined myself. And, immediately, felt like I was swimming in the pool of scarcity. I felt like a bear needing to bulk up for winter.

What happens when we feel like don't have enough? We scramble like squirrels, grabbing all that we can so we don't starve.

Feelings of scarcity can also trigger a release of cortisol, which drops us into that fight-or-flight mode that can make it hard for us to lose weight, manage anxiety, or keep our concentration. This kind of frantic energy is exhausting. This time I decided to focus on abundance.

I put my attention on earning more money as well as celebrating the little bit I could save, instead of what I had to restrict.

If I wanted pizza, or to laze on the couch, or to allow myself to get buried in my work, if I decided to stay up too late, or play small—fine. I was going to do just that. But, at the very same time, I added in other things. Things that lifted me up.

And a cool thing happened: the good habits slowly began edging out the bad. As part of my recharge, I began to add a little tiny bit more activity into my life. I wanted to get stronger, so I'd take the dog for a walk, or drop down to the gym for a short workout. And that left me less time for couch surfing.

I added in a new morning routine, began getting up earlier, and that led me to stop staying up so late, and I began sleeping better. I added more healthy foods to my diet, ate more vegetables, and fewer processed snacks.

Instead of feeling fearful or worried about which new projects to tackle at work, I added in some new things while keeping up with my regular workload. Sure, it took some energy to do this, but also gave me some in return, because I was engaged with things I was interested in. The days went faster, I began looking forward to work more. And my creativity expanded, my interests and opportunities grew, and my enthusiasm soared.

By adding in the good, some of the bad habits just slowly fell away. Nearly without me noticing, they were replaced with something else that I wanted more. Something the made me feel better.

Rather than feeling guilty for my indulgences—like pizza—I enjoyed every darn slice and the salad that I added too.

We spend a lot of time in life trying to cut out our flaws, bad habits, weaknesses. That is constrictive, draining. But when we focus on enhancing our lives, expanding into what feels healthier, and creating an abundant life, we just simply don't have space for anything that doesn't align with that higher energy.

The Habit Three-Step

Habits, good or bad, follow a typical three-step pattern. We are triggered to something, and that spurs us into a routine behavior, where we are rewarded. Food is an easy one to explain. When I'm bored or stressed, I'm triggered to eat high-carb snacks (routine), like a fistful of crackers, and that calms me (reward).

In our Recharge Plan, we can use this pattern to trigger feel-good habits to boost our energy. For example, when I wanted to ramp up my creative expression, I began writing in my journal every morning. This primed my mind to come up with some unique ideas. I'd jot them down. And then start playing with one. The reward is that every time I do this, I feel excited, like I've done something meaningful. My energy increased. And the time spent writing meant less time scrolling through the apps on my phone, an energy drain.

When I begin feeling stiff behind my desk, that stiffness triggers me to stand up and walk around the house, practicing gratitude with each step. The reward is that I feel better physically and more connected spiritually. I'm also more appreciative and less stressed.

Trigger—Routine—Reward.

Don't worry about cutting out your bad habit—at least don't start there—but do pick a few that will elevate your energy and add those in.

Changing our habits to grow and improve is key to vitality and well-being at all ages, according to Margaret Moore, codirector of the Institute of Coaching at Harvard-affiliated McLean Hospital. "Feeling good and energetic requires a daily investment in self-improvement, which begins with letting go of unhealthy habits and engaging in healthy ones."

As you make your Recharge Plan, what are some of the things you want more of?

I added in more movement. More fun with the family, playing cards and stuff. I wanted to add in more fruits and vegetables and more creative work. So I slipped them into my schedule. Some I wrote in as part of my daily plan, like my morning writing routine. Others, like the gratitude steps or playing cards with my kid, I do when I'm triggered and the time is right.

And in the end, some of the things that had been siphoning my energy off for years just fell away. Others became easier to release. When an unhealthy habit did come back into play, I had more resources and more motivation to let it go. Because I didn't want it to get in the way of the things I was doing that felt so much better.

CHAPTER 12
EASY-PEASY

There is this attitude in Western culture, once glorified by the robust adventurer and President Theodore Roosevelt when he said, "Nothing is worth doing unless it's hard."

For a long time, I was attached to this thinking too. If it mattered, it had to hurt. Require long hours at the desk or gym. Now, I think that's hogwash. That rigid thinking is just another energy drain that persuades us that power and force are the only way to get anything done.

It's a philosophy that convinces us that we are supposed to be disciplined, pushing our bodies to the brink, even when they are sick and hurt. Working extra hours even when it's no longer productive. The idea that we are weak if we do what comes easily or naturally, or that it doesn't matter if it isn't hard, is reinforced by our culture. We celebrate the struggle.

But here's the thing—life is hard enough without us piling on. There is plenty in life that doesn't feel good. Things we aren't prepared to deal with, things we are afraid to face. Hurts. We certainly don't need to create more hard moments with the things we choose to do in our days.

Work doesn't have to be hard to be meaningful. You don't have to sacrifice to help others. Marriage doesn't have to suck. Love doesn't have to hurt; health doesn't have to be a struggle.

Life can be fun. The things we choose to do can feel easy and fulfilling—and still be meaningful. We can choose to be around people who make us feel good. Work can be interesting and enjoyable and still pay the bills. This is what flow feels like. And we can cultivate it.

First off, let's take a look at our schedules. Are we making our days harder by overscheduling, or pushing too hard, sacrificing our self-care, gossiping, or complaining about all we don't like?

Are we eating junk, drinking too much, not sleeping enough, not asking for the help we need? There are myriad ways we diminish our experience and drain our energies. I used to complain all the time about how busy I was. How much I had to do, like it was some badge of honor. But it just meant I wasn't taking care of myself. I was busy, but what I was doing didn't matter much.

Now, I'm deliberate with my schedule. Each day includes things that feel easy and interesting. There are stresses and challenges, of course—like the days before a book is due. But I'm seldom stuck in the hard spots.

Because I'm no longer forcing things. I just don't want to spend my energy doing that. I'm not focused on people-pleasing or doing things simply to fulfill the expectations of others. I give as much attention as I can contributing to things that I care about. My family. My work. My friends. My health. Contributing to the community. Living my values. So when I spend time doing these things, everything else feels easier. More satisfying.

Stop the Fight

I am done pushing and striving. I no longer go to bed feeling bad that I didn't accomplish things because I'm accomplishing the things I care most about first. My energy is aligned with my authentic nature and that just feels good. The great irony is, of course, that I'm getting more done with energy to spare.

Consider this. How effective is it to nag or force your teenager to clean the bathroom? How sustainable is it when you never allow yourself to enjoy your favorite food? How well does it work when you try to persuade your aging parents to quit driving or downsize before they are ready? How about stopping a tidal wave, how well does that work?

We spend energy forcing things to work, yet force rarely gets the outcomes we want—and it never feels satisfying, especially when we are trying to enact growth in our own lives.

Recharging isn't about forcing ourselves into a protocol or a one-size-fits-all system. It isn't about pretending we always feel good, or that we are never tired. It's about paying attention to the things we are experiencing so we can add in more of the behaviors, ideas, activities that fill us up, rather than those that leave us drained and clinging to the edge of the couch at the end of the day.

For me, that means I am not going to garden. I'm just not. It hurts my body. There are worms. It makes me dirty. I don't know much about how to care for a plant, or what shrubs to plant where. Working in the yard always leaves me feeling frustrated and tired and achy. I have done it for years because I thought I should do it. It's what grown-ups do. Well, not this one. Not anymore. It was forced every time.

Cooking a good meal for my family on the weekend? Most days, that feels like a better fit.

When you are developing your plan to recharge and feel more vibrant in your life, take a look at your daily calendar. Are you spending time on the things that best fit your interests and abilities? Are you challenged and excited by at least some of the things you do every day? Are you filled up or defeated and depleted at the end of your day? Are the things you are doing adding to your energy, or stripping it away? What are you forcing?

Then take a minute to evaluate what you can quit, renegotiate, regroup, realign. I cook dinner, for example. My husband works in the yard, which he prefers. It all gets done without feeling forced.

Figuring out the coding to develop my own website? That felt forced. It drained the energy and time I had to put into other things, things I enjoyed, things I was actually good at. When I finally hired a designer, I was immediately recharged by the relief I felt. And, in the extra time I had, I took on another project and covered the costs of that website.

And some things, some days, I just let go altogether. I don't worry about whether I can do it all. I'll tell you straight up, I don't want to. I no longer want to do it all. I want to do whatever enhances my life. This way I have more energy to give to others too, and that keeps this whole energetic circle going.

This kind of alignment doesn't mean your path becomes easy and the weeds disappear. Nope. They'll still be sitting there in the middle of the path. But they won't be in your way. You'll walk right on by, sipping a Sonoma chardonnay.

Difficult, Not Impossible

Even the things that come easily to us require consistent effort over time. They need attention. Nurturing. And as we evolve and naturally push our own boundaries, we'll run into corners and walls, have to turn around and backtrack, redirect to figure things out.

That's okay. Research indicates that we are more satisfied and fulfilled when we engage in something challenging, but not impossible. That exploration, the effort to improve at the thing we can't completely master, intrigues us. Those are the things that often stir passion and contribute to valued relationships. We usually don't find the things we can master all that interesting. They are fun and done. We also lose interest in the things that are too hard. It's the middle ground that keeps us going.

This may be why I have been enchanted (and bewildered) by writing for forty years. I've definitely improved since I held a green crayon in my tight little fist, and I continue to learn new things. But there is no mastery. Each piece is like a new invention. Different words and structures, ideas, and information. Sometimes it feels too hard, and I complain and talk about working at a sandwich shop because I love sandwiches. I become surly and pouty. But then I go at it again. Because I can't leave it alone. I want to figure it out, the story, or the book. The idea. I want to understand. Process. Learn. See what happens next. And so I go back to it and, each time, I get a little better.

When you develop your Recharge Plan:

Look for those things that intrigue you. Challenge you. The things you can't leave alone. Things you've always wanted to try. **Write them down.**

Now curate your list of goals and to-dos. What matters? What habits will you put in place in your day that fit naturally in your schedule, what essential chores must be done, and which ones allow you to apply your interests, talents, skills most efficiently? Since it's a myth that we can do it all anyhow, spend your time on the things that seem to flow. This is about fitting, not forcing.

Then add to the list the activities, hobbies, ideas you want to try or learn more about. Your areas of interest, like learning to cook French cuisine, might be difficult to do, but rarely will you have to force yourself to practice or try something new. There is energy in this kind of participation and engagement.

See the difference? Golf is hard for me. Writing is hard for me. I don't always do them well, but once I get going, I need no other motivation. I'll pick them over just about anything else.

Streamline the Process

In our efforts to reboot and recharge, we've got to get rid of the systems that require too much energy without a good return. I used to drive thirty minutes in traffic to get to a dentist. He was a nice guy. Good dentist. But there is a good dentist five minutes from my house, and she comes recommended too. I had my records transferred. I'm not going to spend my energy commuting.

The gym? It's 1.52 miles from my house. I wouldn't go if it was any further, seriously. Most of us won't.

Data gathered from 2017 and later shows that people who live within five miles of the gym exercise more often. Regular gym-goers are willing to travel about four miles, according to the market research firm Dstillery. If it's in a specialized facility, like a barre class, people will drive a little further. But the longer the commute, the fewer the visits. Those who go most often drive less than four miles. Anything more than two miles, I'm out.

I order groceries mostly online because grocery shopping depletes me. When I go out to run errands, I do them all at the same time, once a week. I schedule my phone calls, doctors' appointments, and tapings all first thing in the day, usually on the same day of the week, so I don't have as many interruptions on the other days.

Interruptions drain our physical and mental resources. Each time we are interrupted on a task, it takes about twenty-three minutes and fifteen seconds to get back to what we were doing. According to researchers at the University of California, Irvine, frequent interruptions cut what we can do in a day by 50 percent or more.

The act of shifting our physical body and our focus and concentration multiple times between multiple people or tasks is taxing. Our energy ricochets and drops. By the end of it, if you are anything like me, you're worn out, feeling like you've been pulled in many different directions and gotten little done.

When I'm streamlining my approach with the must-do chores and tasks, I have more time and attention for things like golf, reading, exercising, and writing that bring an energy return. While I may still be tired at the end of the day—after all, giving out effort toward anything takes energy—I don't feel empty or depleted, I am satisfied. Full. Buzzing.

There will always be those things we must do that don't excite us, things that take energy without offering any. But when we create a schedule that makes time for those things, we won't lose as much energy to poor coordination and interruption. That gives us time back to do more of the things that help us recharge.

Look at your schedule this way:

- What must be done?
- What do you want to do?
- How can those two things merge or intersect?
- What can you add to your day that uplifts you?
- What will you do today to make a positive contribution?

Then, look at your answers. Do those things.

Persistence Sticks

When I began with this new easy-peasy scheduling model, I got a surprise.

I was more persistent. I didn't have to push through my day, I wasn't anxious about finishing one thing to get on to the next, I wasn't running all over like a circus clown. I knew what I wanted to do, and that's where I directed my energy.

In the past, I was so scattered by the meetings, all planned during different blocks of time on different days, that it took more for me to stay focused. Tapped out my self-control and discipline.

These days, I'm not looking to quit. I have fewer decisions to make and I had an easier time making them.

One statistic repeated on the internet is that we make about thirty-five thousand decisions a day. What to wear. What to eat. When to go to the store. What to watch. What to write in the email. And I'm not even talking about what happens in a buffet line.

Each decision we encounter requires our attention and energy. The more choices we have, the more self-control and discipline we need. Decisions zap our energy. Even now, I can get to the end of some days and feel completely overwhelmed by the thought of making another decision. I used to feel that way every day. But going with the flow, instead of forcing things, feels so much better.

Our Recharge Plan needs to include time to restore our energy after we expend it. Time for us to do the practices, add in the activities that help us regroup. Think about this today. What will you give your time to? How can you schedule the essentials so that they don't deplete you? What can you add to ignite your energy and recharge? What things will you say "no" to, so you can say "yes" to others?

CHAPTER 13

IF, THEN I'LL DO IT

We could go with tacos. But then we always have tacos. Salad bar? Don't feel like chopping a gazillion ingredients. Takeout sounds best. But it's Tuesday, and a guy named Gareth delivered my groceries, and *if* it's a weeknight and I have groceries, *then* I cook.

This If/Then strategy helps me keep my plans easy-peasy and on track when I don't feel like making dinner or writing the proposal or doing anything else.

To keep things simple and sustainable and to avoid pinballing our energy all over the place, it's best to avoid the fatigue caused by overthinking every freakin' detail of daily life.

I'm an expert at overthinking. Not only does rumination increase stress and pain, it also causes mental exhaustion that can keep us from healthier, happier things.

When I get caught up in overthinking, I feel like a house caving in. Dilapidated. Like the protective outside walls are pressing against my heart, pushing through my car. Too many decisions can trigger this for me. Too many things to do and not enough time to do them can make me feel this way.

If/then planning helps me deal with these energy drains and it's part of my Recharge Plan. It helps me integrate the schedules and practices and the activities and fun I want to have in my life, without adding to the overwhelm.

This technique takes the decision out of the deal. It makes my restorative actions automatic so I am no longer victimized by my own excuses—at least not as often.

Obstacles in View

When it comes to making sustainable changes, the flex and stretch of life can feel daunting. There is always a new app, a new need, desire, distraction, or an old belief to keep us from cultivating the practices that will help us reinvigorate our health and well-being. We say something like "welp, life got in the way," when we don't take the trip or write the book or rebuild the deck we wanted. And it does. But if we let that happen often enough, if we let the distractions rule, we will be moving toward what we don't want. That's depleting. Then that becomes our life.

These distractions are the essence of the obstacles we face. And they chip away at our self-control and self-discipline. It feels easier to skip the workout or put off the meditation for a day. It feels better not to tack one more thing onto the sched—even if it's a good thing. Often, it even feels selfish to take time out to do the watercolor, or sit quietly and read, because you can hear your partner out there doing dishes or a friend calling to hang out. But it's okay to take a breath and pause. Good to let others do what they do, without you needing to be involved. For now, your job is to stop overthinking and create a method that helps you cut the distraction and stay focused on what you want to do to reenergize.

Here are some ground rules.

1. Tell anyone you live with that you are going to be taking time, each day, to take care of you. You don't have to

defend or excuse it, just let them know that, instead of coming home from work and cooking dinner right away, you are going to, say, take a walk, or meditate, or do something else restorative.

2. Choose three healthy things you want to add into your schedule each day or each week.

3. Write these things into your schedule *first*.

Once you've got that mapped out, consider what kept you from doing these things before. Research by Gabrielle Oettingen and Peter Gollwitzer indicates that, if we contrast our desired goals with the barriers that get in the way of attaining them, then we are more likely to stay on track.

One of my goals—to help me get unstuck—was to move my body more. This was not a new idea. I'd tried it before, but my exercise practice fizzled, usually, after a couple of months. I needed to understand why.

Bottom line: I don't like exercise. It hurts. It's hard. Too time-consuming, and just a hassle. Knowing the obstacles we face helps us overcome them, say psychologists.

My new goal was to work out four days a week. I'd identified the barriers to that. Now, I needed a cue—a trigger that would get me going even when I came up against those barriers and didn't feel like exercising. This would eliminate any decision-making. I wouldn't have to think. The cue has become my gym clothes on the dresser.

Gollwitzer says to choose a "goal-relevant situational cue" followed by a "then" that is your desired behavior. These are known as implementation intentions, and they work because they create a connection between an environmental trigger or cue and the desired action. In time, those actions become automatic—habits—that can power up our days.

Here's how it works for me: If it's a weekday and my exercise clothes are on the dresser when I wake up, then I exercise. I put my sweats and T-shirt out the night before. So when I wake up, there is nothing to think through. No decisions to be made. It took about two weeks for this habit to really take hold, but I'm still doing it two years later.

Here's another way to look at it.

What is something you'd like to do more of each week because it's healthy, fun, makes you feel good, or allows you to be more productive or energized?

Why aren't you doing that now?

What cue can you choose to help you overcome those barriers and motivate this energizing behavior?

Write it into an if/then statement.

For example, you want to go to bed earlier? Listen to inspiring music? Learn a language?

If it is nine o'clock, then I will go to bed.

If it's lunchtime, then I'm going to listen to ten minutes of uninterrupted music at my desk.

If it's Tuesday, then I will study Italian for a half-hour online.

If you have a plan in place, *then* you can accomplish your goals.

As you establish your Recharge Plan and start to paddle back from the burnout you've been feeling, use the If/Then strategy to add energizing or healthy behaviors back into your day. Choose activities that inspire you to lean into your talents and curiosities, develop your well-being. Soon enough, you'll feel vitality emerge.

CHAPTER 14

SMALL WINS

In the wintery gray of a Wednesday morning, I lay in bed evaluating each moving part. Ankles achy, but moving. Knees, good to go. Hips. On fire. Stiff with sleep.

Well, let's do it.

In the way that the old song says the shin bone connected to the knee bone, knee bone connected to the hip bone, I work my way through each joint, stretching and unfolding, trying to loosen myself up. From the edge of the bed, I push myself up until I can feel my weight on the balls of my feet. That's what I focus on: the small moves, the sitting up, the standing up. This is how I get through one of the toughest parts of my day. One small move at a time. Most mornings, it feels like I'm tethered to the bed by a million tiny Gulliver threads. Joints locked. Trapping me. I get tired of pulling against them. But getting up is a victory. And I do it. Then, I make my bed.

And by the time I'm lurching down the hall for my first cup of coffee, I'm all in. A woman who gets shit done. That is the power of small wins. And any planning to overcome fatigue and boost well-being must pay careful attention to them.

Since reading the research from Teresa Amabile, small wins are a part of every plan I make—even with the simple stuff, like cooking dinner, coordinating my workday around my teen's orthodontist appointments, or getting gas, I'm always noting the incremental progress I'm making.

We lose our way when our ideas get too lofty, the steps too vague. Wind up feeling bad, when we work all day and record little progress. Often the most meaningful things we do—spending time with our kids, encouraging a friend through a hard time, building a business—don't yield any measurable results for the day. We can get lost, wondering if what we are doing matters at all.

It's hard to stay motivated when our goals might take months or years to achieve.

Sitting on the couch, stuck, in those early months, it was easy to think about where I wanted to be. Fit and forty pounds lighter, with a couple more books published and bluebirds circling around my head chirping light happy songs helping me to dress.

But, when my mind dropped into what it would actually take to get fit (hours at the gym), or lose weight (salads), I felt heat seeping up from the base of my neck, pressure around the collarbone, and I begin to feel beaten before I started.

To circumvent these feelings, I played with Amabile's approach and began noticing and celebrating the small successes.

Like making the bed. No matter what else happens, at least I got up and made some progress in the day.

Incremental progress. Small wins.

What Is a Small Win?

Just about everything we do has multiple steps involved. And it can be taxing to look at all that needs to happen to recharge or lose weight or get the promotion, or write the book, or make the meal. But we can't sit down to a five-course meal until we prepare each individual ingredient. We make dinner one step at a time. And each step is valuable and necessary; each one matters to the entire meal.

Instead of focusing on the end result and the time and effort it will take to pull this meal together, we can start by buttering the bread, and marking that off the list. Incremental progress. Then we tear the lettuce for the salad and marinate the meat. And as we accomplish each small step, we get closer to finishing the feast. But when we stop and notice our progress along the way, the completion of each small step, we get the buzz from the small win. That energizes us, motivates us, builds our momentum, carrying us forward into the very next task. And closer to our ultimate goal.

A marathon is 26.2 miles, but you only have to run one at a time. A book is sixty thousand words, but you make progress by starting the first chapter. Start small. Acknowledge the accomplishment. The small win. And you'll feel better in a big way.

I used to have these wild five and ten-year plans. I'd get all excited thinking about them. But once I got to work, I felt burdened. So much to do. I grew stagnant under the weight of all the steps. Thinking about a whole book, for example, overwhelmed me, but thinking about the first page felt exciting.

I recognized that, if I can keep my focus on today, then I can do the things today that will not only make me healthier and happier right now, but also help me create some small successes so I can keep moving toward my bigger goals.

Anything else keeps us stuck. If you want to lose fifty pounds, that feels heavy in mind, body, spirit. But what if you lose a pound a week? You'll drop your fifty in a year. Small wins. Big results.

Every morning I wake up stiff. If I had to figure out all the mechanics behind what I need to do to walk down the hallway, I'd crawl back in bed. But all I need to do is tip forward a little bit. To tip into a step, shifting my momentum enough to move me forward. That's how we get moving in life. That's how we reengage and revitalize, by drawing in energy and joy one little step at a time.

We don't have to do it all. Just incremental progress. Just lean in a little. Celebrate that step. And momentum will build.

Picking Up the Win

"I was feeling like I was spinning my wheels, so I made a list of everything I accomplished this year so far, and you know what?" Kelly said during our call. "When I wrote it all down and actually read it, I realized I was bustin' moves. I just hadn't noticed."

Recharging isn't about treading water or staying in space, it's about getting things done. Purposeful action. That's energizing and hopeful because we feel as though we are contributing something when we do something that matters. The size of the accomplishment doesn't matter. It's the progress we make.

What move are you bustin'? How will you notice and recognize your small wins as part of your plan to rev up your zest for life?

I keep simple notes of my daily successes on my to-do list. My progress isn't sexy—paid bills, ordered groceries, ate a salad instead of chips for lunch, taped a podcast, took notes on a new book—but this has helped remind me that, even on the difficult days when I feel like I've gotten nothing done, I still made incremental progress. I'm still moving forward. That helps me regain momentum for the next day.

I make a few notes on some of the bigger benchmarks I reach—finished new logo design or wrote three chapters. At the end of the year, I look back and see how all the little steps are connected to the bigger goals. Losing three pounds a month, thirty-six pounds for the year. A few chapters a month turned into the book you are reading. And getting up and making my bed has helped keep me moving. Small wins remind me of what I'm capable of. Nothing is wasted. No matter how slow, how small the progress.

Pull out your journal, the napkin, or the box that your wine came in, I don't care, and drop down three things you accomplished today. Anything. Doesn't have to be sexy, or profound, just has to be done.

Then, tip your hat to your progress and your power. The things we do today will change our lives for tomorrow. The status quo keeps us stuck. Small wins help us amp our power. Make it part of your Recharge Plan.

CHAPTER 15

THE PULSE OF EMOTIONAL ENERGY

When you lift a weight, say, a bicep curl with a fifteen-pound dumbbell, or a jug of milk, or, umm, a 1.5-liter magnum bottle of wine, you can see the tissue in your bicep pulse and push as the fibers come together to create the energy needed for the lift.

Of course, these muscles get tired after three, or fifteen of these curls. But it's when we rest that they restore, grow, get bigger. Giving us more energy.

This is how it works with our core energy too. If you are surrounded by people and things and environments that demand your energy but you seldom take time to replenish or restore or recover, never pausing to let your own energy grow, you don't get stronger. You get tired. We need to take time away from the energy drains for our energy to build.

Years ago, I was acquainted with a woman at work. She was interesting, could talk about anything. She had a hilarious dry wit. But I always felt drained after our long conversations.

I'm an introvert. Maybe the one-on-one was too much? Though I liked her, I never wanted to be "stuck" with her. I decided to pay attention and figure out why. It didn't take long. While this woman is talented and funny, she spends most of the conversation complaining. Detailing what's wrong. Turning down every new solution or offer of help. She talked of bad men and out-of-touch friends. She complained about the food and the weather. Her jokes always at someone else's expense.

It was her negativity that was draining me.

Positive gatherings can tire us too, because of the excitement and emotional charge of connection. Unlike my more extroverted husband, I need quiet time after these social gatherings. But after a fun evening where the energy swirls like stirred paint and ideas and stories and laughs and love and connection are exchanged, the rest time makes me stronger. Rebuilds me. My energy grows as I regroup. In these moments after exposure to uplifting people and experiences, it's not fatigue we feel, but comfort and ease. Belonging.

Places of Expansion

One reason to cobble together a loose Recharge Plan is to create more of these kinds of moments. To create the spaces and environments that engage us and get our energy swirling again. A plan helps us to balance our energy expenditures, like the kind that occurred with the low-energy friend, with the kind of ease that comes from high-energy people.

You move into the places and hang out with the people where energy is expanding. Then you lean back into this plan for balance like you would lean on training wheels. The ideas will keep you upright, but with the right activities, people, places, you won't have to work so hard to pedal.

Slowly, and I know you'll find this too, the positive charge from the things we are deliberately adding in takes on its own energy. It becomes naturally easier to eat well when we are working out. I get new ideas for my work when I'm talking to people who are excited about theirs. More time moving outside means more feelings of awe, which leads to stronger connections and warm feelings.

We have to be willing to surround ourselves with positive, high-energy people, stimulating environments, compelling activities, and inspiring ideas, and filter out those that don't add to this energy. We must say 'yes' to the uplift.

So, when I ran into a friend in a coffee shop and she asked me to serve on the committee to help feed hungry kids in our community, I said yes, even though I was dragging tired and busy with work. Because being a part of an effort to raise the energy for our community, just thinking about it brought me joy. I began eating better, exercising while listening to enlightening podcasts. I moved toward the positive energy, inspiring people, healthy habits, beautiful views, nature and love, and laughter that picked me up. I took care to pause and savor the beauty and goodness. To notice.

And I became more aware of the things that took too much from me, like a negative individual or messy house. The more comfortable I became with feeling awake and alive and good, the less willing I was to let that go. Just as you don't get strong muscles from sitting on the couch, you don't build healthy and vibrant emotional energy by participating with people and activities that constantly suck up what you have to offer.

You build emotional vibrancy through the give and take of interactions with people who are excited and engaged and loving and funny. You go looking for this kind of energy, you leave space open for it, and when you spot it, you bring it in.

Create the Conditions

Inspiration is not contrived. It cannot be manufactured. It strikes. But we can create conditions that make it more likely, says Scott Barry Kaufman, humanistic psychologist and coauthor of *Wired to Create. Unraveling the Mysteries of the Creative Mind.*

Load up on interesting ideas and perspectives. Books, music, podcasts, people. Be open to new ideas and experiences, chase your curiosity, and continue to learn. Spend time talking with funny and interesting friends. Surround yourself via in-person meetings, Zoom conferences, online classes—anything that gives access—with fascinating folks. Take field trips. Poke around on country roads. Invite variety into your life.

The way to emotional growth and energy isn't to stay isolated, but to deliberately surround yourself with the people who are true and authentic and awesome and funny and wise and creative and bright and willing to share all that goodness.

So, who are you hanging out with? Don't judge others—that's draining too—just notice. Are you spending most of your emotional energy doing things with people that fill you up? Build that muscle? Or those who are leaving you frayed?

You'll know. Your body will tell you. Stay close to the people bringing the best energy and yours will arc.

And what are you bringing to the party? Are you sharing your love and humor and joy? Are you meeting others with compassion and curiosity? Are you raising them up too? Energy doesn't just flow in one direction. The most powerful relationships, the most positive ones, are an energy exchange between two engaged and compassionate people.

Choosing Energy-Building Activities

Same with the activities you choose. Creative work, exercise, cooking, playing an instrument, learning to juggle or paint or can peaches—require an energy outlay. But if these things excite you, they will also fill you up.

Creative expression is a big-time energy igniter. It's difficult too many days, sometimes scary, sometimes befuddling. But you cannot make anything unless you are immersed in the process. That engagement is energizing. It can often put you in the flow zone. It is illuminating and insightful and meaningful—and sometimes heartbreaking.

When I'm not coming up with new ideas or work, when I'm not writing, I don't feel good. I feel slow and restless. Off-balance. I don't always notice it at first. Just feel out of sorts, but my husband will notice. The guy who sometimes fails to find the milk in the fridge has noticed that I'm grouchier, more irritable, when I'm not writing.

Satisfaction comes from making something that didn't exist moments before. And then again, when we share it with someone else and it goes out into the world. The energy expands, like one of those compressed sponges that plumps in water (I love these)—it triples in size. Elevating others. Becoming a salve. An inspiration. Art does this. Books do this. Good food and comedy and paintings and movies and music do this. Making stuff does take energy, but in the end, it generates more.

Exercise too takes an energy investment, but your body responds with endorphins and other biochemicals that actually improve your mood and your health and enhance well-being. You get energy back.

When I was feeling stuck, I wasn't doing any of these energy builders. I was doing what had to be done, what I felt I should do. What I had always done. Any energy I had left drained into the couch cushion. Soon, you start running in a deficit. This feels like you are in a bunker of burnout and exhaustion. The first moment you decide to do something better, fight the sense of fatigue and malaise, with a gratitude practice, or stress management practices, or doodling, or laughing with a friend, or dancing like a maniac to ABBA in your living room—just saying that's one option—your energy will spark. Soon it will reignite.

At this stage of your Recharge Plan, it's time to get clear on a few of those people and things that will ignite that spark. What is it for you? How are you tending to your core emotional energy? Are you doing activities that challenge you intellectually and emotionally, things you feel are meaningful, satisfying? Even when it feels challenging, are you invigorated at the end—or defeated? Are you conscious in your quiet time, so you can restore, regroup, rest, and refill? That means taking moments to experience awe, to savor a sip of coffee, or a beautiful sunset. To meditate or become mindful.

Running on Empty

Somedays I get close to empty. It's okay. Energy is fluid. We are going to hit some lows. My family often feels it first. I'm irritable. Sarcastic. Withdrawn. I might feel headachy, or stiffer in my legs. Low core energy reverberates through our minds and bodies.

I freak out over super important things (read: dumb stuff), like someone forgetting to turn on the dryer or another empty toilet paper roll. This mood usually takes hold when I've given too much away during the day without taking time to replenish. My reserves are overdrawn. Then, little inconveniences inflate into big, black, balloons of troubles.

We must catch ourselves here in this emotional space. Notice, in our bodies and moods, that we are tapped out. Then take steps to restore before we go too low and become stuck.

On a low day like this, I try to escape and hide out alone in my bedroom for a while. I'll take a shower. Get in my pajamas, if it's evening, and crawl into bed to read or listen to a podcast or just sit quietly. Other days, I just feel the fatigue, take a good long timeout, and go to bed early. Sometimes I'll go play golf, or pet the dog, or look at puppy videos, or sit out in the sun.

Recognizing these emotional drops requires a degree of emotional intelligence and courage, so we can interrupt our regularly scheduled programming to do what we need to recharge before that internal spark flickers out altogether and moves us into stress and sickness, or disillusionment.

We can be gentle with ourselves, but must take care to keep our energy from escaping through the cracks of hard days and difficult experiences. Energy is our essence, and we must take care to sustain it. Vitality is the life force and the building blocks to everything we want to create in our lives—physically, emotionally, spiritually, professionally, personally.

We can cultivate and care for this energy through lifestyle habits and behaviors and mindsets like the kinds we are developing in our Recharge Plan, here. But we can also pick a few simple strategies to jolt us and provide an energetic edge when we are flagging in the moment. I drop them right into my daily plan and use them when I need a pick-me-up.

What can you do when you need a timeout to replenish and restore? To find your bearings in the middle of the day? Choose a few fast-track energy fillers to use when you need a boost and write them into your Recharge Plan.

Here are five things that help me when I'm running a deficit:

Music. Maybe a little Barry Manilow, depending on my mood, or some fired-up Reba or Dolly Parton country. Beatles, Whitney, Eagles, Yacht Rock—hello, Christopher Cross. I like ballads, anthems, or kick-ass lyrics.

Exercise. I never want to exercise. Always glad when I do. Research shows that physical activity releases endorphins like dopamine and other neurotransmitters that trigger positive feelings and ease pain.

Create. Doodle. Yep. I've been working on a doodle a day. I suck at it, but it's engaging a piece of my mind that interrupts the stress or rumination I've been projecting into other moments. Make something. Food. Art. Essays. Clay pots. Flower gardens. Creating is essential to sustaining emotional energy and creating flow.

Connection. Call. Zoom. Meet someone you can see or touch. It's the eye contact, the tone of voice, and whenever possible, a hug that holds and boosts our good feelings. Social connection is essential to human growth and health. Plenty of studies show it also lowers our risk of depression and increases compassion. Join a club. Sign up for an online or in-person class. Schedule regular visits with friends. This is sometimes hard for me because I like to be home alone. Quiet. Pondering. With my books. But I feel lighter in spirit and mood when I've taken time to connect with others who are excited about their lives.

Animals. Pet the dog. Look at kitten videos. Put feeder out and watch a hummingbird hover. I am mesmerized when I watch my cat clean her paws. She's so efficient and practical. No wasted energy. When I see that YouTube video where the lion, now in the wild, reunites with the man who cared for him as a cub, I get goosebumps—it invokes this sense of wonder and awe and that always brings a higher energy.

CHAPTER 16

FLEXING

The T-shaped handlebars have blue-foam grips at the ends and the whole thing folds out with a snap. Ready to ride with the push of a button. This silvery kick scooter was a present for my forty-fifth birthday.

I went for a ride pronto. Hair poking through the helmet, wind in my face, I was gliding around the cement track at my daughter's school. Right up until that front wheel hit the lip of the track. The scooter stopped. I didn't. Slingshotted into the air, I experienced that slo-mo effect seen in movies. I was in the air just long enough for awareness to dawn. Shit.

With a body full of rigid joints and brittle bones, I knew I was going to break if I hit the hard ground. I also knew I wasn't excited to explain to the ER doc that I'd had a catastrophic accident—on my kick scooter. My best option was to relax into it. Let it go. Hoping that maybe I'd walk away with bruises instead of breaks.

Just relax. Let it go. Don't brace yourself. Be flexible. Fall into it. I hit the ground like a sack of potatoes.

"Oh my God!" my husband, yelling from fifty feet away.

"Mommy. Mommy. Are you okay?" My daughter, skidding to a stop, dropping her scooter close to my head. I could feel her breath on my ear, cheek.

"Mommy."

/ / /

Chronic illness doesn't allow much flexibility. Medications at eight in the morning. Noon. Eight in the evening. What I do on Wednesday impacts what I am able to do on Thursday, so I plan ahead. If I am going to go grocery shopping on Wednesday, no vacuuming on Thursday (too bad). No golf or date night either. I'm too achy and tired. A long day at the desk Monday means a time schedule to stretch and move Tuesday. I keep a strict schedule so I can do what I want and need to get done.

It doesn't hurt that I'm a wired, Type A, organized list-maker, house-tidier, and desk-cleaner. The lack of mental and physical clutter helps me stay calm, productive, efficient. But living this way can contribute to fatigue.

So now, I'm learning better how to let go. To be adaptive, agile, responsive. Creative. It takes an exceptional amount of energy to hold so tight to life. To stick to the routine, one way of doing things, in a world where everything is in flux.

When we let go, though, we can relax a bit, and put our energy into what's in front of us. Unceasing rigidity underlies burnout, and it isn't super fun for the people we live and work with. Agility is an energetic expense too, but the returns can be higher.

Agility is a term business leaders love to sling around. It means we are better able to move with ever-changing circumstances. We are more responsive and engaged, able to flow with any fluctuation. Instead of resisting reality, we absorb it. We begin to work with it, innovate, create, make it our own. It doesn't cost us as much energetically.

To be agile in spirit and action, we have to be willing to let go, relax into the fall, trust that we are capable of managing wherever we land. Because, as we all know, change is the one thing we can count on. An agile response allows us to tweak things to create the next best response, feeling, opportunity.

If we sit around waiting for the agent to call on Tuesday, or the woman to ask us out, or the friend to set up dinner, or the client to show up with a new business opportunity, if we wait for the gym to open before we start exercising, if we always wait for others to lead the way, ask if we are interested, tell us what we are going to do, we will get stuck living life on others' terms. This is depleting. Research shows that people feel better, more positive, and engaged when they have more autonomy. We want to set the terms. We can't always do that, of course, but our response can make them a whole lot more interesting.

This Is Agility

Agility is where innovation lives. And curiosity. Because when something goes haywire—hello pandemic—we can either sit around waiting for life to "return to normal" or we can create a new look for ourselves, and live a good life now with our "new normal."

It doesn't mean we won't grieve some of what we once had. The loss of what we'd hoped for. Of course we will. Loss is part of living. But even within those feelings of disappointment and sadness, we can trust in us, and our ability to respond in new ways to create opportunities.

We can let go of expectations—ours and the ideas others imposed on us. Instead of holding tight, staying rigid and unbending while the world morphs, we can soften a little bit. Fall into what is now.

There is no right way to respond in life, only different ways. Agility allows for discovery. New possibilities, fun experiences, surprises, silliness—our days become interesting. We might feel bruised sometimes, but never broken.

This is mostly how our daughter and I approached remote schooling during the pandemic. It wasn't our first choice. We felt sad. She missed her friends and the hum in the hallways. I missed never being alone. Like ever.

Sometimes home learning was hard and messy and noisy. We didn't know how to do it. but in that not knowing, we also had an opportunity to add in some cool things. Like snacks. We have killer snacks. And sometimes we play "Don't Stop Believing" on breaks. We are shifting to our circumstances and finding ways to elevate.

We can stay in the upset, or we can flex and adapt it to make the moment that's given to us into something new. Flex and stretch.

I used to be thrown by big changes. Now, agility is something I celebrate—and even brag about, when I find a creative way of solving a problem, from the smallest detail to the most grandiose achievement.

Bad hips mean I look a little lopsided when I approach the golf ball on the tee. Sometimes I can't even get up there, and my husband will have to help me. But, once I'm over the ball, I've adapted my swing rotation to make it work so I can keep golfing. And keep playing well enough to beat him on occasion. It doesn't look the same. But it works.

I'm a short person in a house of high shelves, and I have elaborate devices rigged on broom handles and tongs where I can reach up and poke and shimmy those paper towels forward on that top shelf until they fall into my arms from twelve feet up.

It's become a little bit of a family joke around here, because if there is something I want, I'll figure it out. Of course, we can all do this, find ways of bending and flexing and moving and creating to shape our lives and circumstances in ways that feed our energy. We can let loose a little, knowing that we don't have to oversee everything, don't have to tinker with it all, to make it work. Earth will still orbit the sun, even if we take an afternoon off.

That doesn't mean you're always facing ideal circumstances. Managers change, the economy fluctuates, new leaders are elected, jobs are lost, marriages end, companies go bankrupt, and people fall into despair. Some among us revert to complaining, gossiping, refusing, denying, and inadvertently sabotaging themselves.

I've done this too. But then I become curious about how to flex into this new circumstance. If this is what we've got, how can we make it good?

Easing the Ache of Change

Change can drain you. Or you can draw energy from the novelty or the variety it offers. That can be fun and interesting, and that's where the spark turns to fire.

It also means you can drop the tough-guy act at the door. Self-discipline, control, and willpower are no longer the most important qualities on the log-ride of life. Agility is. Resilience is.

Employers want to hire people who can adjust and adapt. Those who are emotionally intelligent, able to reframe and weather upset. Creative folks to guide teams through uncertain times. Our families need these qualities too, to help us in our everyday response to a tumultuous world.

Your ability to bend like a sapling and still stay rooted is particularly attractive in a world where change is constant. And those who can flex with a new idea, system, approach, diagnosis, or circumstance are built to last. When you become that, you have energy to spare, because you invest less in worrying about change.

Agility is a component of resilience. Confidence and courage manifest in the deep knowing that comes when you recognize that you can sway in the earthquakes of life without crumbling.

When considering your own Recharge Plan, think about ways to practice your own agility. Energy withers when we cling to the status quo, trying to fit into a structure that no longer fits by denying that things are different, or aren't working, or aren't right. That's fight and force and depletion.

Energy expands and spreads when we align with our dynamic nature. When we open our minds to other possibilities, recognizing the inherent gifts and flaws of all people, and recognize our shared humanity. Doing things the way they've always been done is stifling. Narrowly judging others because of background or history or color or gender or expectation—or anything—douses the fire. Limits all of us. Agility, openness, compassion, kindness, civil discourse, that's what the fire needs to grow. That's how energy expands.

This doesn't mean that you've got to love the shift and sway. Doesn't mean you'll agree with everything. Both change and agility are uncomfortable and messy. Baffling. Nuanced. But denying that they're necessary is a quick trip to burnout and stagnation and loss.

But agility requires you to show up, become present, and manage your thoughts and feelings in a way that allows you to move forward into a new space with curiosity and kindness, says Harvard psychologist and author of *Emotional Agility* Susan David. When we do that, we align with our own values and desires.

David says emotionally agile people have the skills and resources needed to thrive in our fast-changing world. They demonstrate flexibility in dealing with complex situations and can better handle stress and adversity.

In contrast, the emotional rigidity of black-or-white, good-or-bad thinking can send us reeling into damaging thought patterns and behaviors that make it harder for us to cope.

Agility doesn't demand that you sweeten every side of the situation; it allows you to see and feel it all—even and especially the ick—and at the very same time, you can acknowledge the silver linings.

For me, this is where curiosity becomes a superpower. When I'm bewildered—and I'm a mother, so that's just about all the time—when I'm feeling frightened or dejected, I get curious about these feelings. I start asking myself questions. What do those big-time emotions look like and feel like in my body? What do they reveal? What can I do with them? The minute we start noticing and questioning, curiosity takes over, and then we become engaged in our experience. Energy follows.

Living Anyway

When you decide to be agile, your nerves settle a little, you breathe a bit deeper, sleep easier at night. Instead of feeling like a live wire, the energy within stabilizes so you can respond in the most appropriate ways.

This is a product of trust—some call it faith—in yourself. It comes with practice. With couch courage. When you are sitting quietly, and you start thinking about something new, or how to be on your own, or how you will handle a family crisis, you go to the questions rather than the anxiety. You think, "Hmm, I wonder who can help me with this?" Or "What would it feel like to give this thing a try?" Or "What can I do now to make this better?"

Then you feel afraid, and you've got to lean into the fear or conflict. To do what you've never done. You make excuses—I'm too old, I'm too broke, I'm too tired, I'm too sick—and then you get up anyway. You do it anyhow.

When you live life anyway, you don't deny the fear or the uncertainty—you just do the things that matter more, anyway. Because you decide to trust in your ability to figure it out. To survive the try. To enjoy the process. To become braver. You choose energy and engagement and growth to guide the next fifty years of your life, to step in where people need help, to trust that doing is more important than sitting wondering about what you could have done. The living is in the doing, in the being. Life is finite. There are clear beginnings and endings. The outcome is the same for all of us. What counts is what we do between the beginning and end.

That's why agility had to be part of my Recharge Plan. It prevents me from getting derailed by the ups and downs. Reminds me to go with the flow, and to stretch and flex and persist when obstacles appear.

This meant moving from the more planned and predictable life I'd followed to a more flexible mindset. And really, as I've been working on that, it feels more exhilarating, because you never know when the magic will arrive, but it always does if you go looking for it.

How to Practice Agility

Believe that you are a person who can handle change. You might not like it, but developing a mindset that supports your agility will help you navigate through the inevitable ups and downs.

Recognize your feelings. Susan David recommends creating some distance between you and the emotion. You might "notice" your heart is beating fast or you are feeling scared or frustrated, but that doesn't have to be all you identify with. You don't have to *be* frustrated; just notice that you are *feeling* frustrated or the situation is frustrating.

Look for ways to match your desires with the new reality. Facing a new reality—one that you didn't want and don't welcome—isn't easy. And it's a sure way for fatigue to flair. But when you can find a way to match your new reality with the things you still value and care about, it builds resilience. And that is your place of power.

When school was canceled during the 2020 pandemic, it was shocking and disappointing. But my wishing it wasn't happening didn't end the pandemic. Didn't prompt district officials to throw open their doors to welcome my daughter in.

We grieved. Complained a bit. I felt nervous and overwhelmed at first. Not long, because after a while it just becomes too tiresome to stay stuck in the upset. Then, really within minutes, we both started thinking about the possibilities that are also inherent in any situation. I was excited to have more time with my teen—though she wasn't sure this was a perk. She realized she could sleep in longer, move during class. We've fit some fun things in between her online classes.

We adapted, not by denying the difficulty, but by recognizing the possibilities within it.

Getting Up Again

My cheek was flat against the dirt of the unraked baseball field where I'd vaulted over the scooter. The wheel of my daughter's scooter was still spinning where she'd dropped it. Now she was leaning close to my head.

"Mommy?" Her hands petted my hair.

The points where my crumbling hips connect to my pelvis pulsed. My elbow throbbed. But even as I was lying there in a heap, my scooter upended three feet from where I'd landed, I thought, "Wow. I was riding a flipping scooter!"

I knew this was going to be a great story to tell. A great story to write. You know the one, about how the tired, bored mother got off the couch to go for a ride. The one where she crashed. She thought she'd break, but instead, she relaxed and let her body become pliable. Flexible. Instead of shattering. She got up. And went for another ride. It wasn't pretty; she had dirt on her cheek. But she got up again. Bruised, but not broken. You know this story. It's your story too.

CHAPTER 17

ADVERSITY VITALITY

Our terrier is a ten-pound tank when she plants her paws. Like she has now, rooted in the middle of the bed, the flat of her head pushing me toward the edge, into another morning.

The sun hasn't yet cracked the sky and the air is damp, chilly with rain. The dog is hungry and I don't want to move. But I do. I get up, slowly loosening my achy body like a carpenter's rule. But by now you know this is me. Arthritis has challenged me, but it isn't an obstacle in my life. It's a part of my life.

When we recognize that adversity isn't some failure or mistake or flaw, but part of being alive, we can glean energy from it. Hold our heads up. See the tough stuff coming. Look it square in the eye, and step into it knowing we will be changed, but not diminished. Knowing that because we are agile, we can take the intense energy of the bad stuff and transform it into something better.

A melanoma diagnosis years ago made me healthier, because I scheduled regular skin checks and caught other spots I wouldn't have noticed. Tricia Thompson took the fear and intensity that came with learning her daughter had epilepsy and let it motivate her to build a business helping other parents with kids who are struggling. Fred Guttenberg's daughter Jaime died in the Stoneman Douglas High School shooting in 2018. He is now a gun activist transforming this shattering experience into one that is making the world safer for the rest of us.

Nobody wants this kind of pain, trauma, adversity. It may be the hardest thing we ever do? But it does not have to render us powerless. The energy around adversity can become resilience—messy, imperfect, tearful, heart-pumping resilience that will then carry us through the next storm.

There is energy in movement. In surviving the unsurvivable, or even just getting through a shitty day. At every bend, we must deliberately decide to keep going. To get up, find meaning in the awful, take an action that will help us keep taking a breath, and create the next part of our experience—even when we are bruised and hurting and angry.

This is adversity vitality—the energy and power that somehow trickles in when we think we have nothing left. When we wonder if we are too broken, or tired or scared or pissed, to go on. Our adrenaline surges, and our thoughts align so that we can rise up, do what must be done to heal, recover, help, get through, rise.

And when we remember our strength, our resilience, our skills, and our abilities, when we remember to love even when we are afraid and to laugh at the absurdity of it all, we get stronger—for always, not just now. We become less afraid. Softer. More open. Vital. And that energy becomes action. And our actions become focused on the rebuild. And soon we have.

Daily Drains

It's not enough to transform the life-altering adversity. Any plan to recharge must include managing our daily diet of stress as well.

Glitching technology, traffic congestion, long commutes, work pressures, and relationship challenges—the daily stresses—

weigh heaviest of all, according to Carolyn Aldwin, director of the Center for Healthy Aging Research in the College of Public Health and Human Sciences at Oregon State University. Aldwin and her team followed 1,300 men over twenty years and found that 64 percent of those who viewed their daily lives as hassle-filled and full of everyday stressors died earlier. More than half of the men who described their lives as stress-filled died.

Those who claimed to have fewer hassles had the lowest mortality rate. But here's the thing: Those men, the ones who lived longer, experienced the same stressors and upsets as those who died. The same ones. They just explained them differently.

"It's not the number of hassles that does you in, it's the perception of them being a big deal that causes problems," Aldwin explained. "Taking things in stride may protect you."

"Right now, I am angry and afraid," a friend told me after a family member relapsed. "I'm afraid that I'll have to make some tough choices. I also know I'm too tired to process rationally, so I'm settling in, and settling down until I have more reserve. But this time? I have absolutely no doubt that I have laid the groundwork to deal. Not once have I said, I can't deal with this or I can't live like this. It's all been, I will *not* live like this. That is my power."

If we view our everyday stresses as problematic, unfair, upsetting, overwhelming, they do in fact erode our mental and physical health, making it hard to cope and sleep, contributing to our overall fatigue. Recognizing them as part of life can shield you. That is our power.

Remember? It's how we tell our story that determines how we experience our lives.

///

It was a winter-dark night on the highway, and I was stopped, waiting for the truck ahead to turn left. A car was coming toward us fast. Headlights blazing. When it was only feet away, the truck in front of me turned. The collision shook my car.

The truck was tossed, twisted, into the ditch on the other side of the road. The other car was facing the wrong way, the driver's side crumpled. But the driver managed to wave and signal that he was okay. I turned on my hazards, grabbed the flashlight under the seat, and ran to the truck in the ditch. The driver's head was thrown against the steering wheel. Blood was flowing from his forehead, over his brow. I leaned in. "Hey, you okay? Wake up." Heard him moan and saw his shoulders rise with a breath.

There were no cell phones then, so I drove up to my parent's home a thousand feet up the road. Called 911. Grabbed blankets and water and lights and we went back to comfort the men, help however we could, and talk to the police. Within a couple of minutes, other cars had stopped. Police arrived. I spoke to the officers, provided blankets, waited for the ambulances. I was a college kid, never seen anything like it, but I felt calm. Methodical. Thoughtful and efficient in my response. Going through what I'd been taught to do in case of an accident, step-by-step. I had all those tools in the back of my mind, and they showed up when I needed them. I felt prepared. Not panicked.

Until I got home. And sat on the end of the bed in a dark room, alone, and began to tremble. Felt the fear settle in, the discomfort of seeing a body broken. Of being so close to death. I was filled with empathy. Then, after a bit, those feelings passed into awareness, and I moved on. I've thought about it since, sure, but not with any anxiety—just with awareness and the knowledge that bad, hard, scary, shocking things are apt to happen in this life, but we can gear up, get ready, develop the tools to deal instead of being derailed.

Create a Bounce-Back Kit

A Bounce-Back Kit is a mental stockpiling of the practices and approaches, the physical and psychological skills, that can help you work through daily setbacks and big-time adversities.

Just as we get our water and canned foods and flashlights together in an emergency preparedness kit, in case of fires or earthquakes, we pull together relaxation processes, emotional management techniques, and problem-solving skills in our Bounce-Back Kit to help us manage stressful times.

Knowing we have these tools available takes some of the pressure off, some of the worry out of living. Helps us be proactive. That allows us to put our energy into rising up, rather than getting dragged down.

The best athletes in the world have practiced ways of doing this, too. Injuries are a significant threat to anyone who plays a sport and can end a career in an instant. Researcher Dave Collins looked at how athletes respond.

He evaluated those who are at the top of their games and found, unsurprisingly, that many are internally motivated to play and improve.

But the difference between them and other players was in how they managed adversity. Those at the highest level of their sport view career-threatening adversity more positively. Instead of being diminished by their pain, fears, challenges, they are proactive, energized, and more motivated to work hard and come back better.

The second-tier players were surprised and unprepared for adversity. They were shocked when it happened. And they were more likely to quit and fall apart, rather than recover and work to heal and improve.

People. We are not second-tier *anything*. We are proactive, empowered. We can prepare and gather our resources now to help us through the hard times later. This is part of our Recharge Plan.

Qualities to Add to Your Kit

There are a lot of skills and practices and qualities you can toss into your emotional emergency preparedness kit to build your resilience. Your kit could include optimism, humor, growth mindset, social connection, and agility, of course. Emotion regulation, gratitude, self-confidence, and capability. Perspective, or at least the ability to reframe. Macaroni and cheese doesn't hurt either.

What's key for your Bounce-Back Kit is that you know how to use these tools, and you've identified your strengths in advance. I'm good with a growth mindset and curiosity. I'm a seeker of silver linings and have good support. I'm not as good at steering myself away from ruminating thoughts. So, to keep me out of trouble with those, I use curiosity and mindfulness exercises. Consider the resources you have, your unique strengths, attitudes, and abilities, then put them in play.

Six things to put in your emotional emergency kit:

1. Relaxation response practice. Deep breaths, meditation, something that will help you calm the heck down.

2. Cognitive reality check. Find a strategy to help you figure out what happened without all the false beliefs or distortion we often create.

3. Emotion management techniques. Learn how to identify and label your feelings so they serve as a guide, not a hindrance.

4. Problem-solving approach. What now? How will you work through the challenges? Who can you call for help?

5. Perspective. This is where I look for the silver linings. I may cuss at them, but at least I can see they're there.

6. Happy hour or social connection. Super important to have family or friends or trusted doctors and advisors you can hug, vent to, complain to, and share all of your dramatic survival stories about how you clawed back from the brink, preferably while drinking vodka.

Finally, macaroni and cheese. Getting through anything should be celebrated. Find a recipe for your favorite comfort food and use as needed.

Know this: Mac and cheese matters. In all seriousness, comfort foods do comfort, according to a small study led by researcher Jordan Troisi. It isn't the flavor we are craving as much as the feeling of connectedness we get from chicken noodle soup or mac and cheese. Our favorite comfort foods ease loneliness, enhance our feelings of belonging, and can also reduce stress, Troisi found.

Alright. We know the categories we need to fill in our kit; here are some specific practices you could keep on hand.

1. Relaxation Response

Use to Calm or Relax

Five-minute complaints. A friend hosts Shouty Thursday on social media. Anyone in the group can post all-cap complaints, and she always validates and responds. There is something powerful and funny about this form of modern venting. Blurting your troubles out in a single sentence. Find your own version of Shouty Thursday. Blurt out the problem, shake your fists a little, then let it go. Or scribble them out in a notebook and toss them away. Or set a timer, complain for five minutes, then move on. Don't dwell, but don't deny either.

Unplug from devices. Excessive noise and news disrupt our calm and our ability to restore. When feeling pressed, unplug.

Meditate

Do diaphragmatic breathing. Belly breaths from down deep, slow, and steady, ease the fight-or-flight response that can make us more reactive.

Do relaxation exercises. Progressively clenching and releasing muscle groups for ten seconds at a time can relax us.

2. Cognitive Reality

Use to Figure Out What Happened

Evaluate what happened without blame or judgment.

Sit quietly in solitude to contemplate or meditate on the challenge.

Avoid personalizing. Create some distance from the situation by evaluating it from a third-party perspective, says University of Michigan researcher Ethan Kross. This can help us gain some clarity and self-regulate.

Acceptance. Deal with what is, not what you wish was.

Stop using absolute words like never, can't. That's a sign that you are catastrophizing. And the added stress that causes won't help a bit.

3. Emotion Management

Use to Not Freak Out

Label your feelings. Get specific. Kristen Lindquist, an associate psychology professor at the University of North Carolina, says that labeling our emotions stimulates the prefrontal and temporal regions of the brain that help us understand and regulate our feelings. When we give a label to our emotions, then, we can diffuse their intensity and make it easier to deal with them.

Stay focused on now. I know, the advice to stay present is getting a little woo-woo cliché, but it is so helpful, because most of what we worry about hasn't even happened yet. And it probably won't. 85 percent of the things we stew about never occur, says clinical psychologist Melanie Greenberg, author of *The Stress-Proof Brain*.

Yet worrying about the what-ifs can create other problems, so stop it. Put this into practice in your Bounce-Back Kit and stay present.

4. Problem-Solving

Use to Address the Mess

Go looking for solutions. Your agility and creativity kick in to determine the next, best right action. Resilience grows through action. Do something that might make the next moment a little better.

Find evidence that you are capable of dealing with the tough stuff. Remember the last time you were in a mess? Well, you handled that just fine. You'll be okay—believe it.

Sleep. Eat. Move. Take care of your body's basic needs so you have the energy and mental clarity necessary to meet the challenges ahead.

Give your attention to the positive things in your life. We are complex, multi-dimensional beings and can hold the good and the bad all at the same time. Don't deny the bad, but it's okay to focus on the positives too, even during the toughest times. Find the good things. Savor and enjoy them. And the tougher stuff will be easier to manage.

5. Perspective

Use to Improve Your Options

Reframe the situation. I think of this as "getting a grip." If you are anything like me, you've gone through every little detail about what's gone wrong, about a billion, gazillion times. Let's switch it up and take another look. View the challenge another way. Instead of telling a bad-news story, what are some of the benefits? What can you learn? How can you help? In other words, find the silver lining. Make it into a quilt. Even if you have to use duct tape to do it.

6. Happy Hours and Connection

Meet your friends. For a coffee or beer, or a glass of wine, and a good cry. Connect with the people you love, however you can, and share and laugh and listen. Ground yourself in their good energy. Seriously, there isn't much this doesn't help.

Get professional help. I love therapy. Not even kidding. You get to go, talk about your stresses for an hour, and receive coping tips to boot. Many therapists take insurance or offer a sliding-fee scale and payment options. Love it. Do it. Eighty percent of people who felt stressed, anxious, or depressed found greater happiness, satisfaction, and productivity after working with a therapist, according to the American Psychological Association. I'm one of those 80 percent.

Join a support group. You don't have to be lonely in your challenge. We have all been there—wherever there is. Seriously. Others have encountered the same challenges you and I now face. Reach out, we can help each other through it.

Join meet-ups or clubs organized around your interests. Golf, pinochle, tai chi, cooking, plein-air painting, bowling, and books—there is a club for just about everything. Find one with like-minded people who like what you like. The connection is empowering, and resilience-boosting, and it's important to keep doing the things you enjoy even during times of adversity.

Ask for help. Seriously. People. You need help (we all do), and we also need to be the helpers. Research shows that the people who help others feel even better than those who receive the help. It's a gift to all when we lean on one another. Ask for the help you need. Later, you can be the one helping others.

Threebies

Yesterday I walked out of the office after a twelve-hour day. It was six o'clock. My husband was sitting on the couch reading headlines on his phone with one eye on the football game. My daughter heard me close the office door.

"When's dinner," she yelled from her room. "I'm hungry."

I felt this rush of emotion come through my ears. My throat clenched and I opened and closed my right hand. Wanted to storm around upending furniture and punching walls.

Seriously. I'm in here working and you guys are lying around and you're asking me about dinner?

But I was already tired. And I didn't want to hurt my hand and have a mess to clean up. I didn't have the energy to give to the drama, so I just leaned my head against the wall in the hallway and waited for a minute. A minute and a half actually. Ninety seconds. And the feeling, the storming-through-the-house intensity I'd felt a minute earlier, eased and changed into something not as angry and hard.

Emotions do this. They flip the switch, light us up, and then they dissipate. In about ninety seconds. I talk about the physiology behind this more in Chapter 30, but for now, all you need to do is hang on. Just let it roll through, instead of behaving badly and making things worse. When we can do that, we end a lot of stress and heartache. I don't even put this tip in my Bounce-Back Kit. I carry it around in my back pocket and use it. All. The. Time.

It's one of three things I use when I feel myself getting caught up in big fear or anger and need a quick resilience booster. These threebies might work for you too.

1. **Hold on there.** Take a deep breath. You will feel different in ninety seconds.

2. **You have all you need to manage this moment.** You don't have to figure out your entire life in the next thirty-seven seconds. Though, I have tried. It doesn't go so well. You only have to do right now. Take the pressure off. Just do now.

3. **Difficult does not mean impossible.** Goodness gracious, just because something is hard doesn't mean you can't handle it. Of course you can. We are so layered, have so many tools at our disposal. Everything we need to get through the tough times. Don't spend your time thinking otherwise. You might not know how to do it yet, but you'll figure it out as you go.

When we are buried in things that feel hard, we get tired. Stress is depleting. Sitting for hours in a hospital, working through the terms of a divorce, laying off staff, processing a shocking diagnosis, figuring out how to pay the bills when the paycheck is still days away—this stuff can leave us fatigued, frustrated, and more than a little afraid. Some days I even feel overloaded by the mound of dirty clothes in my closet. But the tools in our Bounce-Back Kit do help us build resilience and give us some tools we can use in the upset to protect and preserve our energy and stay out of trouble.

CHAPTER 18

MOUNTAINS AND MOLEHILLS

I can't remember when I first heard it—it was always just a Mama Mantra. Frequently repeated. Particularly when I was an eighth-grader prone to dramatics and a Shakespearean angst marked by you-don't-understand-anything shouts.

"Don't make mountains out of molehills," Mom would say. A polite way of telling me to get my shit together.

I still use it today to remind me of the importance of perspective. So I leave it here for you now: "Don't make mountains out of molehills."

We are talking about getting back on the road after hitting a midlife rut. Our energy can flourish in conditions of contrast. We get a charge from the combination of negative and positive forces. And that helps us grow.

But if we take a scattershot approach, casting our energy out everywhere, we will find ourselves facing fatigue and burnout again and again, feeling as though we have too much to do without the time and resources to do it.

We must be discerning about when and where we direct our energy because, once released, it expands, casting particles into ideas and opportunities and fun, or drama and struggle and challenge. If we lob it in the right direction, we can use it to manifest magic in our lives. Not even kidding. Put it out there. But, if we lose that focus, it will diffuse, and bring us down too.

Mountains and molehills. It's important to know the difference, so we don't lose all our strength and power and momentum to the molehills.

Abuse is a mountain. Addiction? Mountain. We need to put our energetic resources there first to become safe and healthy. To restore our well-being so we can recoup the vitality that is lost to violence and hurt and illness.

Pursuing your biggest dream? Mountain. Living your ikigai? Mountain. Nurturing your relationships? Mountain.

Being criticized at work? Molehill. Too much to do, not enough time? Molehill. Running late on deadline? Molehill. Hair going gray, your candidate not elected, finding a lump? Job loss? Molehill. Molehill. Molehill. Molehill.

It's hard, I know, to distinguish. Mountains—like recovering from a serious illness—require our focused and immediate energy to traverse. Molehills can be big-time stressors, sure, but there are lots of paths we can take to manage and move around them.

Even with something scary and hard, like finding a lump or getting a divorce, there are processes, protocols, and people who can help us access the treatments and resources we need to be well, even while navigating the molehills and parenting our kids and working our jobs.

We can manage many molehills at a time. Mountains require more of our energy to climb.

Don't Make Mountains

The thing is, we often give the same amount of attention to the molehills as we do our mountains. For example, a week after I was diagnosed with melanoma, I was waiting for the oncologist in an exam room. It was a long wait. I was cold, naked under my gown. And the longer I sat there, the angrier I became, because who did this guy think he was to disrespect me and my time?

Later, exhausted, I realized how much energy I'd given away, during an already stressful time, to the molehill of the doc's poor time management, instead of the mountain of my melanoma treatment.

Jeez Louise. Nobody loves a mole. But, unlike mountains, we can move over the molehills.

To recharge, we must be discerning in how we allot our energy. Direct it toward the places that matter most. The things that help us create and heal and contribute and uplift and inspire ourselves and others, not the slights or annoyances or inconveniences.

We just don't have the time to bother with molehills. We just do not.

CHAPTER 19

OPTIMAL DISCOMFORT

None of us start out being stuck. We start out busy, animated, in patterns of growth that have us scrambling to figure out a new job, or how to feed the baby, or how to pay for a roof repair, or how to plug in the software. And it's hard because we aren't all that familiar with any of it. It's all new. But then we learn. We get better at it with practice. We relax a bit. The baby grows up, the roof gets fixed, the first few months of a new job turns into the first few years of a career, and we are so grateful for having weathered all the initial discomfort, all that growth. We settle in and enjoy the comfort and familiarity.

But after a while, the routines and patterns that felt so comfortable begin to feel, well, boring. We are restless. Stagnant. We don't realize it until we stretch just a bit—maybe we see an ad for an exotic vacation locale, or we read something interesting about snowshoeing, or get offered our dream job—and our fingertips touch that place of possibility.

We think, oh, that's interesting. That might be fun. Might be worth a try. And we stretch a little further and move into a new space, and it's exciting and exhilarating and energizing and so darn scary and uncomfortable because we are on the very edge of what we know, about to fall into something new.

This is optimal discomfort. This is a place that drives our energy and growth and curiosity and action. It's where we discover our purpose, learn who we are, again and again, fall in love, create art, parent our kids, quit our job to chase a dream. It's the gap between what we know now and the unknown of what's next. And it's an essential aspect of our Recharge Plan because when we become easier with uncertainty and discomfort, we don't deplete our energy resisting it.

Instead, we recognize it, observe it, and take in the new energy that helps us grow into great things.

The Middle Zone

I think of this as my middle zone, the stage between the I'm-dozing-through-life phase and this-is-so-hard-I'm-dying-here phase. Optimal discomfort sits right between the two, when we encounter just enough novelty and challenge to keep us curious and engaged, but not so much that we feel inadequate, like we can't function or move.

Growth from this place might leave us feeling a little nervous or jumpy, but it's also invigorating. Fun. Engaging. Feels like anything is possible when we are in that place of optimal discomfort. It's active.

We do new and different things. Meet interesting people. Talk about different subjects. Experiment. Do the things we've always wanted to do. And that feels good. Novelty boosts well-being and satisfaction.

Feels like hitting the golf ball on the sweet spot or pinpointing the ideal temperature where the bread begins to rise. Like when your child shares something special with you, or you meet a new friend. Of course, you must still swing the club to hit the ball, and hitting a golf ball is tough. There is a good chance you'll miss the mark altogether. Your first loaf might fall into itself. But it's okay, because you are learning and experimenting. And that's both exhilarating and uncomfortable. Optimal discomfort.

Think of a skier standing at the top of a black run, looking down, knowing in her mind's eye that she has the skill to complete the run, but not knowing what the conditions are like, or what she'll find at the bottom. Despite that, she trusts in her ability to adapt as she goes and have a good run.

Growth does not happen when things are fixed. It occurs when our brains must adapt and expand, develop new neural pathways to deal with unfamiliar tasks and conditions.

There is a time for this fixed living. Time to restore and regroup and reboot. A time to reflect. To evaluate what worked, and what didn't. To create a plan like the one we are working on now.

But it isn't all the time. To ramp up our energy, we must be willing to move to the edge of our comfort zone, into the space where we are more thrilled than afraid, but honestly, feeling a bit of both.

How do we know when to press into optimal discomfort?

When we feel stuck. When tomorrow's schedule looks exactly like today's.

When we are wistful and tired. When our comfort zone isn't comfortable anymore.

Then we know it's go time.

CHAPTER 20

GO TIME

"I feel so deflated," a friend texted, after seeing the tax bill for her emerging art business. "I made so little and it seems like all that effort wasn't even worth it. Sorry, I'm grumbly today, going to get some coffee and pick myself up off the floor and get going."

Yes. First coffee. Then action.

After we take a beat or a week or whatever time we need to identify what's catching us up, the very next step is action.

Feeling bewildered, burned-out, disappointed, disillusioned, is not unique, nor particularly interesting. But it is so real. So human. We all experience these feelings. They are universal. And even when you've found the things that amp up your energy and good feelings, you will still have shitty days. Days where it's all a slog and you are mad and tired and enough already.

Even on these days, though, we haven't lost the spark. The pilot light is already burning, ready to whoomph when the gas is turned on. But you are the one to hit the switch. To get up and make a move toward the kind of life you want. Because once that initial energy is organized into a singular beam, a consistent force, it's like the sun in a magnifying glass—it only gets more powerful. Now what?

We've identified the problem, the factors draining our vitality we have a plan in place, a structure to guide us as we recharge. Now we need to get up and do it.

Get up.

It is hard to stay stuck in disappointment when you are moving. And it's the moving that creates the storm, a whirling tornado where our actions create the energy that elevates our moods and builds physical strength. Then we throw that zip into our next dream, goal, plan, action, and our energy grows and the cycle continues.

I have to remember that actions infuse energy when I'm dragging. When I feel tired or beaten down by circumstances, I have to remember to just get up and go toward the job or emotion or hobby or self-care habit that aligns with what I want to feel and contribute and experience in this world.

Say "yes" to the project, make time to exercise, pet the dog, or write the thank-you note. Get going on a bucket list or draft the chapter, paint the picture. Make art. Or call for support. Just like I do when I can't get started. Just like my artist friend did that day when she was feeling low. She reached out, changed the vibe, and created an energy storm in her own life.

"You can be grumbly, of course," I wrote back. "It is so stressful to do this work. It can be deflating. You worked hard. This is a setback. And, still, it's worth it. You are making art. It is sustaining you no matter what you earn. But it's also sustaining the others who see it. This stuff matters. I know the money stuff is real, but in the long run, it will not be what lingers. You are creating. You are a maker and that brings value to all of us."

"Yes. Okay. I just can't stop creating," she texted. "It's the one thing that keeps me sane."

She said, yes.

We are all makers. Creators that sculpt moments into a life when we take action, when we say "yes." When we keep going.

It's go time. Just get up. Tip into a step and you'll be moving forward.

We aren't always going to feel good or inspired or comfortable. We won't always be glowing with the energy to create this activity or mood or idea we have. Sometimes we are going to feel grouchy.

Action is the answer. Get up. Do something to move closer to where you want to be. Movement creates momentum. It's go time.

PART III

The Practice

Here we go. We know what we want to do—recharge. We have the plan in place, a structure to help us overcome the obstacles and fatigue, amp up our energy, and enjoy our lives again. Now, we've got to get cracking. This is the doing.

The active, science-backed, practical steps, strategies, hacks, ideas, and approaches I regularly rotate in and out of my days to make the moments of my life more positive, engaging, and interesting. The things I use to stay connected to inspiration and creativity. And the practices we can use to launch into the vital lives we want. Lives that feel good and are full of mental, physical, and spiritual well-being fill us with good feeling, the kind that motivates and excites. The kind of daily engagement that brings us alive again.

Best thing about this section? Everything here can be easily dropped into your day or used as one-off ideas that help build awareness, well-being, and health. These practices will help us direct our energies in ways that elevate everything else.

CHAPTER 21

THE BASICS

Sleep. Eat. Move. Repeat.

Even as I write these words, I'm trying to finagle my way around them. They seem so, well, basic. Gotta be something more to this. And they aren't very fun. I mean, I do love to eat, but the sleeping and the moving? Pshaw, I say. Yet there are thousands of studies, courses, programs, psychologists, doctors, and friends, backing these basics up. It's a fundamental principle that, if we are going to do anything well, let alone recharge our bodies, perk up our brains, and infuse our lives with energy, we've got to get enough sleep, eat nourishing foods, and regularly move our bodies.

We've got to tend to these basics like grown-ups. Consistently, like it or not. We do the darn strength training, we eat the broccoli, we make the investment in ourselves.

It's the only way. Believe me. For a long time, I gave little attention to these things. It wasn't until I made them a primary focus that I started to feel better, less tired, more focused. These things are so essential to our mental and physical health and well-being— definitely linked to better cognition, moods, immune function, balance, heart health, longevity—that if we don't give some attention to our physical infrastructure first, we simply cannot spark the energy we need for everything else.

I do know—after some personal research—that one can survive for a good long while on wine and microwave popcorn and no exercise at all. But here's the thing, it just feels crappy. It's hard to focus on work, it's annoying to feel winded from walking across the grocery store parking lot. Who needs that? We get a commercial break of time on this planet and it seems so sad and so wasteful to spend it all feeling physically worn-down. Fueling up on wine, popcorn, and couch time is like driving a 1975, avocado-colored Oldsmobile on a scooter engine.

This isn't new information, of course, but there is a difference between knowing and doing. While I understand the value of exercise and eating well, I'd often go in fits and spurts. Eat salads for a week, work out an hour a day every day for that first month of the new year, then I'd burn out until March. When I'd tackle it all again.

Finally, the irony and the icky feelings caught up with me. I've spent three decades studying psychology, practices, and strategies that we can use to create the thoughts, habits, beliefs we need to live our potential. I was focused on what I was putting in my brain, but not consistently attentive to what I was doing with my body until it wasn't working well.

To get unstuck, I started by eating, sleeping, moving more often. These became the very first things I did. And for a while, they were the only things I did. Because, honestly, I was so burned-out, I couldn't muster anything else at the time. So I did these things better.

And tending to these eat-sleep-move basics began giving me those small wins I needed to make everything else work. These behaviors increased my energy, and within the first week, I had more of it to share.

I'll get into some more specifics as we go forward, but today, just give it a go.

Add in some exercise. Eat one additional serving of vegetables. If you regularly eat five, today, eat six. Zero? Then today, add in one. And make sleep a priority.

Sleep Schedule

When our daughter was a baby, we learned really quick that a consistent, book-snuggle-backrub bedtime routine was the best way to get her to settle down and stay in bed until she fell asleep. Every night at seven thirty, for roughly three thousand years, my husband and I would take turns wrangling her to bed and going through the routine. But, by the time she was five, bedtime was seldom a problem. She was primed and ready to sleep.

Yet, my sleep schedule was all wonky. I'd stay up late reading and then feel exhausted in the morning. Or I'd go to bed early, get up at dawn, and feel worn by noon. Sometimes I'd eat late, crawl into bed, spend an hour scrolling through my phone, then spend another hour freaking out about the news I'd read on my phone. And hellooo perimenopause, that screws sleep up in whole new ways. My haphazard sleep habits combined with the ache of arthritis pain kept me from sleeping well. I rarely felt rested.

Sleep experts would say I had poor sleep hygiene—which sounds so dirty. But true. I had poor sleep habits. No wonder I was waking up tired. Beyond that, poor sleep quality can also diminish our physical and mental health, making us more prone to chronic illnesses like diabetes—lack of sleep affects insulin release and can lead to higher blood sugar levels, problems with balance and coordination, high blood pressure, and increased risk of heart attack, inflammation, memory problems, and mood disorders.

Some other details that got to me? Lack of sleep screws with our focus and creativity and makes us more susceptible to viruses, wrinkles (!), and weight gain. The body's natural chemicals, the ones that signal us when we've eaten enough, get out of sync when we are tired, and that makes us likely to eat more.

Got it. Need to sleep. But it's never come easy to me. Tired of feeling tired, I was ready for a new approach so I revamped my sleep habits to align with advice from medical experts and research from the National Sleep Foundation.

These things might help you sleep better too.

Set a schedule. I go to bed at the same time every night. I wake up at the same time every weekday. This primes my body to rest.

No eating or drinking anything but water after seven o'clock on weeknights. No caffeine after four o'clock, no late cocktails; eating dinner late often leads to disruptive dreams, so we eat a bit earlier whenever we can.

Keep the sleeping space cool, dark, and quiet. We rarely turn on a TV. Our space is dark. Sometimes we'll crack the window. The key is to be comfortable—not too hot, not too cold.

Turn off the phone. I try to avoid my phone now, for that last forty-five minutes before I turn off the lights. I do read in bed for about a half-hour, which is not a popular idea with sleep experts, but works for me and helps me unwind from the day.

My schedule changes on the weekends, and like any of the practices we use to recharge, it's okay and can be necessary to move any of these practices and personal habits around, so they work for us without becoming an added stress.

I can't always eat an early dinner or go to bed by ten o'clock, but for me, this is the ideal schedule. A consistent mark I try to hit. And I feel so much better when I do.

Do what works for you, play with this a little. Create your own sleep schedule. Adapt it to fit your comfort. Then try it for a month. It will feel rigid in the beginning, but your body will catch on and you'll get better at it. It got even easier when I added regular exercise.

I still don't like to go to bed. If I could function without it, I'd stay up and putter, and ponder, and howl with the coyotes. But I can't function, or even talk to people nicely, if I don't sleep. It doesn't work—for any of us—at least after the age of twenty-three.

To recharge, regular sleep is a must. Learn to do it well. Zzzzzzzzzz.

CHAPTER 22

THE BLOODWORK

She flicked her fingers against the tender spot on the inside of my arm, looking for a vein to rise. I clenched my fist. And unclenched. Still, no clear line. My skin here is laced with pinprick scars from all the blood tests I had as a child. Blood tests to look at the SED rate and other markers of inflammation.

"Let's give it a go over here," said the phlebotomist, while flopping down another armrest and shifting the chair around in a single movement. The vein rises to the surface in my left arm now. I feel the pinch. I look over when she pops the third vial onto the narrow hose running from my arm. Red, vibrant, and bold, my blood-red against the background of the light sage green chair and the beige floor and the beige walls. I wonder what these cells will show. I tap a silent rhythm in my lap with my right hand.

When I decided to recharge and begin to move, and rest, and properly nourish my body, I knew I needed to get a physical benchmark to understand what was going on in my biology. Vitality is a whole-body experience, and if one thing is off—whether it's the way we rest, or manage our thoughts, or the health of our body—it's tough to energize and feel good unless we give a little attention to it all.

I had a long list of things I wanted to talk to my doctor about. Wrote down the concerns and questions I had, the tests I wanted her to order. She added in a few of her own and scheduled the labs.

Here are some of the key markers we checked through a simple blood test.

Blood sugar: This measures glucose in your body. Too high, your body isn't making insulin or using it efficiently. This is a big deal because insulin moves sugar into the cells to be converted for energy. High levels can be a sign of diabetes. According to information from Harvard University, you want to be at levels less than 100 milligrams per deciliter (mg/dL) on a blood sugar test and a hemoglobin A1C of less than 5.7 percent—whatever that means. Be sure to ask your doctor for a translation and to find out what is right for you.

Lipid panel: Alright, this is the cholesterol and triglyceride stuff. Get this test, peeps, and don't freak—this is directly affected by exercise, diet, and prescription medications, so if you have higher levels and are at higher risk of heart disease, you can do something about this.

In this category, you're looking for total cholesterol of less than 200 mg/dL; HDL cholesterol of more than 50 mg/dL; LDL cholesterol of less than 130 mg/dL (less than 100 mg/dL for women at high risk for heart disease); and triglycerides of less than 150 mg/dL.

Serum iron test: This and others, like the ferritin blood test, measure the amount of iron in the blood and how much is stored in the body. Iron is key to the making of the red blood cells that carry oxygen, and for healthy organs, muscles, and just about everything else. Low levels can mean anemia and crushing fatigue. High levels might indicate aches and pains and liver disease. Test results between 60 and 170 mcg/dL for the serum test are just right.

Thyroid-stimulating hormone (TSH) and T4 test: The thyroid regulates metabolism, which can influence our weight and energy and other stuff. This test indicates whether your thyroid is working right. If it's not, you are more likely to have fatigue, muscle weakness, an increase in appetite, faster heartbeat, and other icky things. But there are ways to treat thyroid issues, including medication, so good to know.

The Results Are In

A day later, the doctor sent a note explaining my results and a summary of my physical.

When you are thirteen, you brag about the grade you got on the math test. When you are a midlife mama, you get a little swagger around good cholesterol and thyroid numbers, so I felt better when she wrote, "Everything looks pretty good."

Thyroid, okay. Blood sugar levels, fine. Cholesterol? Slightly high—thanks a lot, cheddar. The SED rate, or erythrocyte sedimentation rate (ESR), commonly used in folks with rheumatoid arthritis to gauge inflammation levels in the body, was borderline high, but that was expected and not scary.

"But," she wrote, "I'm very concerned about your vitamin D levels. You check in at a nine."

Normal is a twenty. Is this a big deal? Yep, it can be.

The vitamin D test: The 25-hydroxyvitamin D test, if you want to get fancy—measures the levels of vitamin D in your blood. Low numbers are fine, if you don't mind misshapen, brittle, weak bones, more aches and pains, fatigue, and maybe a greater risk of chronic illness, poor immune function, and cancer.

But I did mind those things and, jeez Louise, I was failing with a level of nine when twenty is healthy. As we age, it's harder for us to get and absorb vitamin D, in part because we absorb it from the sun and most of us are heavily sunscreened or not going outside as often. But you can also consume vitamin D-containing foods, like milk and fortified orange juice and fish like salmon and tuna, or add supplements to your diet.

In my case, the doc prescribed a clinical dose for three months. Within two weeks, I felt revived. Seriously. More energy. Better sleep. Fewer aches—which is a huge perk for me. I was so low that the high dose was immediately noticeable. And, after increasing my levels, I've been taking an over-the-counter supplement ever since.

Do the bloodwork. Find out where you are—what your body is lacking and what would help it to function and feel better. Then you can start there.

CHAPTER 23

TWENTY-MINUTE MOTATION

For years, I began the first Monday of the new year like this: Get up at five thirty, put on a new T-shirt—usually gem-colored blue—and head to the gym for an hour-long workout, a routine that I would promise and swear and pinky-swear to maintain every day for the rest of my life and into eternity.

The second Monday of the New Year was generally marked by a thirty-minute workout and self-praise: "Good for you, at least you got some time in. Boo-yah."

By the fourth week? I was a midlife cliché. I had a mind filled with excuses, a body stiff with pain. I'll just take today off, I'd decide. Get after it again tomorrow. The time between tomorrows became longer.

My intention was true. I believed the scores of studies I'd read about the importance of exercise to regulate energy, maintain health, manage our moods, stave off dementia and chronic illness. Heard my doctors talk about the importance of movement to ease stiffness and inflammation. Though I hated exercise, I did like feeling stronger afterward.

I didn't need to be convinced; what I needed was a customized set of rules that I could sustain. I'm a first-born rule follower. I like to know what I'm supposed to do. But exercise was a toughie. I had a hard time keeping up with the recommendations from the experts.

I've read reports that recommend intensive intervals—bursts of exercise combined with brief rests—and studies that say a vigorous hour is ideal for a strong heart. Others recommend an hour of cardio, followed by a half-hour of strength training. Four days a week is fine, or six, I guess. Depends on what information you look at.

I tried for a vigorous hour. My knees burned, hips throbbed. After a few days, I'd quit to recover. The more I moved, the more difficult it became for me to move. The irony of arthritis is that you need activity to stay active, but it often hurts. Too much or the wrong type can actually stop you from moving, too.

Exercise for all of us demands a delicate balance of movement and rest. For me, those ratios change from day to day, so it was hard to find a formula I could keep to. I'd feel good and strong for a few weeks, and then crash. Discouraged, I'd give it up for a few more months of couch-surfing.

This didn't help me feel any better, either. When we fail to move our bodies consistently, our moods take a dive, and we experience more mental and physical fogginess and fatigue.

It was time to break the experts' rules and make my own. Find my own balance, a physical yin-yang. Not a hard-charging, all-or-nothing approach. But not nothing, either.

Your Body Fit

I'm betting you've had your own love-hate relationship with exercise. We hear so much about the right ways and the wrong ways to strengthen our heart and lungs, build our muscles, improve our balance and flexibility. But I couldn't make those ideal practices work in a sustainable way.

I decided, finally, to take what I had learned over the years and shape a routine that worked for my unique body, schedule, and lifestyle. One that would help me get stronger without leaving me feeling disappointed in myself. I wanted a fail-safe workout routine that would build my body, not hurt it.

Here's what I came up with:

Go for four and twenty. I get a minimum of twenty minutes of activity—which can be anything from the elliptical at the gym, to vacuuming the house, or circuit training with elastic bands on the deck, anything that gets me moving—at least four days a week, but never more than six.

If I want to go longer than twenty minutes—which I rarely (read: *never*) did, at least during the first six months—I'd allow myself up to forty minutes total. Nothing more.

At the end, I'd give myself an atta-girl. Instead of feeling bad that I only exercised for twenty minutes, I celebrated by recognizing my effort. And saying it out loud. "Good job moving today."

To help me keep this commitment, I followed the If/Then part of the plan I detailed in Part II. The night before, I'd put my sweats and T-shirt on the dresser. If I saw them sitting there when I got up in the morning, I'd put them on and go exercise first thing. No decision required. If the clothes are out, I go. And much to my surprise, this quickly became a habit.

One that I've followed ever since—more than two years now. While things fluctuated a bit during the pandemic, I've found that this twenty minutes of exercise, done consistently over time, has made me stronger and more flexible than any of the other, more vigorous exercise I've done during the fits and starts over the years.

And mentally, it was freeing. I didn't feel like I had to give a big chunk of my day away to a workout. Nearly every day I'd think, "It's only twenty minutes, I can do that."

Twenty minutes is nothing. Nothing. And everything.

Research now backs up the benefits. Shorter, more frequent exercise is better for our hearts than longer sessions performed less often, according to a study out of Brigham and Women's Hospital in Boston.

Duration doesn't matter as much as consistency, said Dr. Claudia Chae, one of the researchers who studied the exercise habits of more than twenty-two thousand men over twelve years. There was no added benefit to the men who worked out longer than twenty-four minutes than there was for those who exercised for eleven to twenty-four minutes. But the more frequent the exercise, the lower the risk of heart disease.

Maybe my heart is doing better. Certainly, my head is. I feel more focused during the day. Better about myself. That's an energy boost right there. The commitment I've made to regular movement and motation is a commitment I've made to myself. To live this big life I want to live, I've got to have the energy to do it.

Whether you have a chronic illness or not, recharging your body is about listening to it, about providing what it needs it needs so it can supply you with energy. We've got to build it, strengthen it, move it.

When I was a kid, my mom would say, "Let's get motating," when she wanted us to get out the door and into the car.

How will you start motating? What movement will you add to your life to strengthen your lungs, muscles, and heart so they can carry you easily into your next adventure? How will you bolster your body to recharge your life? Will you garden? Bike? Dance to a YouTube video? Walk around the neighborhood? Will you play Wii or Xbox with your kid? The boxing game about ruins me. Exhausting. And fun. Find a game that gets you moving.

Start at twenty minutes a day. Listen to a favorite podcast or audiobook, or playlist. Add more time if you want. Consistent effort over time is the way to recharge, and you'll be jazzed with the energy this creates for your body, sure, but also your mind and spirit.

CHAPTER 24

EATING EVERYTHING MORE OR LESS

Eating More

I like beer and pizza and potato chips and tater tots and burgers and bagels and macaroni and cheese. And I also like quick meals, like cheese and crackers or an apple, that I can grab on the go and eat at my desk.

Call me crazy, but I also love roasted Brussels sprouts, salads with peppers and avocados and cucumbers and radishes. I like turkey burgers and whole wheat pasta.

But to recharge, my eating habits needed some revision. Because, while I'll eat just about anything (except beets), I tend to grab and go. Rather than making meals for myself during the day, I'm a scavenger, prone to eating anything I can easily pull from the fridge or cupboards, or nothing at all until dinner. Then, super hungry, I overeat.

I wanted to clean up my eating habits, put the right kind of fuel in my body, but I knew I had to keep it simple, and I wasn't about to go on a diet. The second I start thinking about cutting foods from my diet, I get nervous. This is why in the Recharge Plan, I mentioned keeping our focus on what we can add to our lives before we talk about what we need to eliminate.

I started by eating more fruits and vegetables. Here's how I did it. I cleaned and prepared the vegetables (locking them in plastic containers or bowls so they were easy to grab) when they first came from the store. And I ate vegetables at every meal. Even breakfast. Again, to help with this, I used the If/Then approach. If there were fresh vegetables ready to eat, then they'd be the first thing I ate at every meal. All I needed to do was have them ready in the fridge.

Then, to circulate them into my diet, I picked go-to items for every meal, venturing into the land of green smoothies. The first day, I felt like I was drinking grass from the front lawn. But I did feel satisfied, and even lighter, after drinking that smoothie. More focused, too. Placebo effect? Maybe. But I liked the feeling. Smoothies became part of my routine.

Here's the recipe I use—as always, keeping it simple: Two handfuls of spinach leaves, or about two cups. Half an orange. Six frozen strawberries. Sometimes a little almond milk, a little water. Sometimes a little vegetable-based protein powder, but not always. I'll pack these up the night before and zap them in the blender in the morning. Dark leafy greens are important here, so pick and mix your faves. Done deal.

For lunch, I'll often have a salad. Usually, I just throw lettuce and cucumber and peppers in a Tupperware container the night before, while I'm preparing dinner, and add tomatoes and avocado and other stuff to it the next day.

For me, it's all about the prep time. Once the foods are sliced and cleaned, I don't mind eating them. I'm fine with a container of carrots at my desk for lunch. So I began making sure I had healthy, energy-building foods available when I did the grabbing.

This is important, especially in the beginning, when we are feeling slow and stuck. We need to stick to the things that require little energy to do, but pack a big return. This was an easy one. And I noticed the difference almost immediately. Here is what I wrote in my journal after a couple of weeks:

"I'm feeling pretty not bad anymore. I don't even hate the smoothies. Huh."

Choosing Power

I was more awake and focused after lunch. Felt better during the day. But the biggest change of all surprised me. After years of never feeling in charge of my body, of living with a chronic disease that was having its way with me, I felt empowered.

Living with chronic disease is like checking the weather reports hourly the week before a lavish outdoor wedding. You wake up each day hoping for a good forecast, with mild weather that isn't too windy. But you know, that coastal drizzle (hello, I live in Oregon, so this is real, people) could blow in at any time. You don't know what the weather will be until the ceremony begins.

Chronic illness also fluctuates rapidly. One hour you feel fine, the next depleted and achy. The experience changes by the minute.

But isn't life like this too? It bucks and twists. So much we can't control. But we can control what we put in our bodies. I can choose the smoothie and salad. I can choose roasted Brussels sprouts and black bean burritos loaded with vegetables.

That shift might actually help me live longer. Research shows that eating more than five fruits and vegetable servings a day reduces the chance of heart attack, stroke, cancer, and early death.

Scientists from Imperial College London reviewed ninety-five studies about fruit and vegetable consumption and found the biggest health benefits come when we eat about ten portions. Five is good for reducing some risks, but ten is da bomb.

Researchers estimate that approximately 7.8 million premature deaths worldwide could be potentially prevented (jeez Louise) every year if people ate ten portions, or 800 grams, of fruit and vegetables a day.

Two-and-a-half portions of the good stuff a day does lower our risk of heart disease by 16 percent, and stroke by 18 percent. But eating ten portions lowers our risk of heart disease, and confers a 33 percent reduced risk of stroke, a 28 percent reduced risk of cardiovascular disease, a 13 percent reduced risk of all cancers, and a 31 percent reduction in dying prematurely, according to the studies reviewed. For that, I'll suck down a bunch of smoothies.

Hydration is key, too. Experts dicker over the amount, but I worry less about the actual ounces and focus more on sipping water all day long. I have a twenty-four-ounce bottle at my desk right now. I also drink a lot of coffee. Not giving it up. Nor am I passing on the occasional evening cocktail. But I've become more conscious and mindful. Coffee is a diuretic; alcohol contributes to dehydration as well. Don't let these and other beverages, like sugary juices or sodas, replace the water your cells need to communicate, repair, and move about the body.

Not only did I begin to feel better when I took in more of these foods, but as my energy grew and my body changed, so did my thoughts.

I began to think I was stronger. Believe I was healthier. On the days when my body was slow and tired, I could still decide to nourish it with gentle stretching for twenty minutes and healthy foods that felt like they were literally infusing me with energy. I began to feel more alive from the inside out.

Eating Less

I powered through the greens, Brussels sprouts (do not judge; roasted, they are delish), and asparagus and peppers. I bought the organic berries and grapes and added more avocados and other fruits and vegetables, and I ate less of other things. Note: I did not say I stopped drinking coffee or wine. I did not stop eating pasta—though we are whole-grainers—not giving up pizza. If I want a potato chip, I'm gonna eat it. But I just began eating less. Of everything.

As I added more fruits and vegetables into my daytime dining, I felt more satisfied. I took smaller portions of other things, not really wanting seconds. I ate a salad before pizza and was filled after two slices. Instead of feeling tired, and tight after dinner, I felt good. Satisfied. Comfortable. And because I was eating more fruits and vegetables, it was also taking me longer to eat. Who knows? I'm a slow masticator or something. But, because I was eating slower, not only did I irritate the teen daughter, but I also became more aware of my body filling up, getting enough.

When I felt good, full, I stopped. Sometimes, that meant leaving food on the plate, and that felt wasteful. That wasn't how I was raised, and yet, I quickly learned to take less food from the get-go.

Recharging isn't about limits, it's about filling up on the right food, ideas, activities, fun. I stayed focused on eating first, the foods that supported my body, and revved up my physical energy. Keeping this in mind, and really feeling the difference, made it easier to keep up these basics until they became habits. Now these habits are a lifestyle.

Eating Everything

When I felt so tired and stuck, I was also stuck in my eating habits. The way I did everything in my life. It was a narrow and limiting way to live. So when I took on this plan—this commitment to myself to recharge—I knew the approach had to be expansive, broad. The plan and approaches had to be open to tweaks and ideas and flexibility, not only so I could stick to it, but also so I could work from a more open and creative mindset. My approach to eating was no different.

At the core of this nutritional reboot was this: I would eat anything I wanted, whenever I wanted. I was no longer going to live a life of guilt and tension. Wasn't going to feel bad about what I was putting in. I was going to be deliberate in what I ate and enjoy it all.

Being alive and vital means putting in the nutrients that help our physical body sustain that energy. But it also means savoring every moment—including the foods we eat.

The times I'd previously decided to diet or eat less to lose weight were rough. I became a little wild. A little Cookie-Monster-ish inside. If I were to think, "I can't have a cookie," all I wanted was a cookie. I felt such pressure. And, when we are already feeling low and burned-out, the last thing we need is to put more pressure on ourselves. I wasn't about to invite more stress in. So, while boosting my nutritional intake with fruits and vegetables first, I decided I would also eat whatever else I wanted, whenever I wanted. As long as I really wanted it.

This was about mindful eating.

One day, after I'd spent hours working to write a complicated piece on a tight deadline, I sent it off, shut down the computer, walked out of my home office, and grabbed a beer from the fridge. It was like a dance routine. I popped it open without thinking. With the first sip, I knew I didn't want it. I'd grabbed it without thinking. Was trying to fill something else, trying to calm down, redirect my energy. It wasn't the beer I was hungry for.

I put the bottle on the counter and thought about what I really wanted. A chocolate chip cookie? A carrot? No way. Was it a hug, a moment of quiet? Did I need to celebrate the work accomplishment or go for a walk?

No. It was never about the beer. Or the food. It was the calm I was craving.

I poured the amber into the sink. I'm more deliberate and mindful about what I eat and drink now. I no longer eat unless I'm hungry. If I eat my salad and two slices of pizza and truly want a third, then I'll eat it and feel fine about it. We are not rationing. But I no longer drop it down on my plate unconsciously without understanding what it is I'm hungry for. This is just about slowing down. Noticing.

This is where you can start playing with your own eating practice. Which foods make you feel physically good? Which feed your brain and help you focus? When does your body most want to eat?

Add in the things that feel good and taste good too. The foods that make you feel sharp and strong. For me, this was never about losing weight—though I did, and that helped reduce my pain and fatigue. It was about nourishing myself better, creating better health so that my body had more energy to support living a wholehearted life.

Ultimately, I dropped about forty pounds over the year, regularly losing about three pounds a month. I put on some weight during the pandemic, because my body was craving different foods for a time and my activities changed, though I still keep to my twenty minutes or more of daily motation. When I found my new equilibrium, began adding more vegetables back into my diet, started eating fewer carbs, and slowed the cocktails, the pounds came off consistently again.

Choosing to let go of both the guilt and the food-centric focus, while being more deliberate and mindful when I do eat, has been refreshing. I don't feel guilty. Heavy. I feel strong. Sharper. Happier. In control.

Eat more vegetables. Eat less of the things that don't nourish your body and brain. Eat everything you want, mindfully, whenever you want. But only eat when it's the food you hunger for. Not because you've had a bad day. Not because you feel guilty for not cleaning your plate. Not because it's mealtime.

Be clear and mindful—not stressed or guilty—about what you are putting in. And you'll find yourself choosing the foods that will lift your energy, strengthen your body, support your mood, and leave you feeling recharged.

CHAPTER 25

GOOD EASY ENERGY

I am grateful for the silver fountain pen that's writing these words. And my hardbacked spiral notebook. I'm grateful for hot coffee on a dark cool morning. I am so grateful for my dog Lexi and my cat Sneakers and little cat Scouty who is pushing the flat of his head against my fingers as I try to write. I am grateful for the way the sun cracks through the clouds. Grateful that my knee doesn't hurt today and I've got leftovers for dinner and enough time to finish my work. Grateful for books and the seasons and my warm white socks. So grateful for my daughter.

These are some of the things I've written on my gratitude list this week. I make a list every morning, adding about five-ish things in. I avoided this practice for a long time, believing that, because it was so easy to do, it couldn't be powerful. I was flat-out wrong. It is easy. It is also one of the most powerful practices I've ever done.

Here's how I do it: In the morning, I take a deep breath, sit quietly, and write down five things I'm grateful for.

Boom. Just like that, I'm done. But it's what happens after I make the list that has the power. Appreciation is restorative. It's a relief, particularly on the days when it's harder to see that goodness that still lingers. On the better days, recognizing the simple goodnesses elevates the moment, layering on the warmth and appreciation.

Research shows that a regular gratitude practice contributes to a greater degree of happiness and well-being. But it also does something else: It untangles us from the toxic emotions that can bury us. In one study, participants who were receiving mental health counseling and writing letters of gratitude to others each week, experienced a significant improvement in mental health, according to Joshua Brown, a professor of psychological and brain sciences at Indiana University and one of the coauthors of the study.

In short, gratitude is good for our minds, bodies, and spirits.

Another study showed that those who kept an online gratitude journal for two weeks experienced a decrease in headaches, stomach pain, skin problems, and other health issues. Robert Emmons, one of the foremost gratitude researchers, found that students who wrote about things they were grateful for felt better and had fewer muscle aches, nausea, and other conditions. Gratitude won't take care of everything. Some studies show no improvement in the health of participants in select groups.

But it cannot hurt. Seriously. What will it hurt to take a minute to amplify the good in your life? To feel good about who you are. To dwell on the upside by appreciating this one life.

Fast Five

Write down five things you are grateful for.

Then choose a new five tomorrow and do it again. And then the next day.

Challenge yourself to find different goodnesses every day, and soon you'll be looking for gratitude in all that you do.

Take it in. Let that good energy fill you up. It may not heal all that ails you, but dang, it makes it easier to keep going.

CHAPTER 26

GETTING UP, GETTING GOING

When I worked in public relations, I had a go-to fir-green suit. I wore it with a silk shirt that had patches of color. Eggplant, indigo, brick red. Each color bordered with a braided gold design. Fancy for a girl who was flat broke and more comfortable wearing overalls. But I was playing the part. Wanted to be considered a prepared professional woman. And something about getting up each morning and putting on a suit made me feel like someone who should be taken seriously.

When I left that office job to write from home, I still got up and put on that suit and a little makeup every morning. This was, of course, crazy, but I was young, focused. Wanting to make a go of it as a solopreneur.

Getting dressed for work in my home office became a ritual. I'd shower. Pull on the trouser socks, the slacks that matched the green of the jacket, tuck in that blouse, add the earrings, drink coffee from a mug with an elephant on it, then walk across the hall to my office in the master bedroom. I did wear slippers, not toe-pinching heels. I hadn't lost all my marbles.

While the suits would change from day to day, my process would not. I was slow and mindful of how I prepared for work.

Thinking about this now, more than twenty-five years later, two things about that time are clear:

1. Wow. I am such a nerd.

2. And, I think it worked.

Putting on my big-girl clothes every morning did prime me for the serious job of building a business. The ritual process of putting on a suit grounded me in the day ahead and helped me stay focused and disciplined in those early days when I had no real schedule to adhere to, no supervisor, no one feeding me assignments. The ritual of dressing like a professional reminded me I was one.

This process made it tangible—not just a dream, not a hobby, a job—and if I was going to make a go of it, I needed to, well, get going.

I stopped this ritual within a month. These days, I mostly wear sweatpants to work. But I still begin my day with a ritual. I call it a Power Hour, and it yanks me out of my slump into a place that feels a lot more fun. Rituals can do that.

The Morning Routine

Rituals have been used by humans for millennia to give thanks for a good hunt, to provide protection in rough waters, to establish a relationship to a god, to marry and bury. To celebrate and grieve and give respect and reverence and significance to the moment. To hype us up and to calm us down.

Athletes are famous for their rituals—watch how a batter prepares to hit, or how a golfer lines up at the tee. And there is some evidence now that rituals do enhance our experience and may even lead to better performances.

In a series of experiments run by Lysann Damisch of the University of Koln, participants were given a "lucky charm" or a ritual process—something to hold, a mantra to say, an action to repeat—to bring about good luck. Those who had the "lucky golf ball" as opposed to the regular golf ball did better. In another experiment, when a researcher said, "I've got my fingers crossed for you," the participant performed better.

Those with the lucky rituals reportedly felt more confident in the task and they gave greater effort, which caused their performance to improve.

Rituals can help us all feel this kind of confidence and keep us more connected and grounded. They can also improve our attention and focus, and even lead to greater satisfaction. One study by Kathleen Vohs indicates that we enjoy our birthday cake more when we go through the ritual of singing and blowing out candles.

Rite-of-passage rituals, like weddings and graduations, shuttle us from one phase of life to another, and help us mark beginnings and endings in a way that creates meaning and purpose.

Daily or weekly rituals, like sitting at the table for a shared family dinner, pouring a glass of wine and toasting your spouse, or conducting a Zoom happy hour with colleagues after work each Friday, are a way to connect us to our life and each other. That makes us feel as though we belong, gives us a greater sense of purpose, emotional stability, and awareness. All of this goes to building our good energy, happiness, and well-being.

Emotional stability and confidence? Bing, bing, bing, bing, that's what I want. The moment I learned about this was the moment I went all in on a big ol' fat morning ritual. And I tweaked mine to boost my vitality.

Here's how my morning routine works most weekdays now:

Six o'clock: Up and at 'em. I stumble to the bathroom. Wash my face. And then meet with the cats who are waiting for breakfast in the garage.

Then, on at least three of the days, I'll do my twenty-minute workout.

Ritual begins at 6:45 when I pour a cup of coffee—yep, this is part of it—then I sit with hands cupped around the mug and breathe in the aroma. Take three deep breaths.

Next, I begin writing my morning pages. Artist and author Julia Cameron's book *The Artist's Way* details this powerful process. But each day I write at least three, handwritten, unedited pages into a brown spiral notebook using my fountain pen.

I end the pages with my gratitude exercise, listing five things. Then I repeat them aloud, head bowed, and I spend a second or two reflecting on each.

A few days a week, I'll follow this with a ten-minute meditation, while sitting quietly in the corner of the couch, feet flat, eyes closed.

Sometimes I'll "study" for a few minutes, reading something about writing or psychology, or another topic I want to learn about, or something that inspires me. By seven thirty, I'm ready for the day.

My morning plan might feel cumbersome to you. For me, it's calming and peaceful because everything is performed with a quiet reverence. No phone. No noise.

Your morning launch will look different. It might take fifteen minutes, include a prayer or a walk or a cup of tea, or rocking out to Bon Jovi. You do you. But do it in a set of deliberate, repeatable steps—same time, same place, same way—with reverence and respect, every time. That's the ritual part of it. It elevates the experience from a habit to something meaningful. Something that will leave you feeling more focused and connected, and vibrant.

My Power Hour can be done anywhere. So choose a ritual that can move with you. I may do it a little later on the weekends, or in a different space so I'm not disturbed. I use it on vacation. Sometimes I skip the meditation or reading. Depends on what is going on that week.

I do take deep breaths, write morning pages, give gratitude—every day. Those three things are the core of my ritual. And a way to nurture my mental, spiritual, physical energies.

This makes for a powerful and intentional start to the day. The deep breaths energize my body. Gratitude connects me to my higher self and boosts my mood. Writing primes my creativity and eases me into my work. Meditation or contemplation roots me in my energy and the energy of the universe and helps me remember my compassion. Reading inspires me.

At first, I didn't want to get up early to do this. Now, I don't want to miss it. I feel edgy and rushed when I do.

Habits are those unconscious behaviors that we do without thinking. They can take us over. Rituals help us live deliberately, thoughtfully. And that enhances our lives.

Taking a Moment

From the moment we open our eyes, how we get up and start our morning will influence how we feel about the day. It's worth curating those morning behaviors, habits, and rituals so we feel good.

For years, I had routines by default. Alarm goes off. I hit snooze. Finally, I get up. I'm late. Wake my daughter. Get her going. Make her breakfast, pack a lunch, remind her to put on her shoes or brush her teeth, take out the dog, send my daughter off to school, go to work. Already feeling tired from the rush, from the doing without thinking.

A morning ritual helps us contain this energy before we give it all away to the day. It's like making a deposit into an emotional, energetic bank account that we can then draw on, instead of starting with a deficit.

My morning ritual gives me my get-up-and-go. But it's also a dynamic thing. It can change and shift as I change and shift. I didn't always write the pages. Some months, I meditate longer and forgo the morning read. One day, I'll change it up entirely, but I'll use some type of ritual to create a powerful morning.

Now, it's up to you. How will you start your day? What will your morning routine look like? Which rituals will you add to power up your day? Be deliberate. Choose activities each morning that build reverence for this life moment you have, that demonstrate respect for your experience and your purpose, and that will help you stay close to that vital power that is your essence.

CHAPTER 27

PAIN DRAIN

When it comes to the practices that help infuse our lives with positive energy, we have to also plug the holes that allow that energy to seep out. We can't keep feeding our souls and psyche if we aren't going to take sleep seriously, for example. It's hard to recharge if we aren't willing to add things into our day that make us feel better, elevated, and excited. Without adopting some practices that help us to build, repair, protect our energy, we are going to leak it like a sieve.

And I've got one cannonball-sized hole that I need to plug. Pain. It's constant.

If you've ever lived with consistent pain for more than a day or two, like while the bones knit back together after a break, or you're healing from pulled a muscle, or have a grinding toothache, or migraine, you know how mentally and physically demanding it can be. It sucks so completely that it's tough to write about it. There aren't words big enough to convey what it can be like some days.

At least 20 percent of all Americans, more than fifty million people, live with chronic pain, according to the Centers for Disease Control. It doesn't matter what degree of pain you experience, or where you fall on the scale. Hurt is hurt, and we've got to learn to manage our pain so we can protect our energy reserves and recharge.

I do a lot of things to manage mine. Movement and stretching. Acupuncture. Physical therapy. Medication. Talk therapy. Sleep.

Meditation. Visualization. Ice packs. Whining and wine-ing. Depends on the day. Depends on dozens of variables. One thing is clear: managing your pain must happen both in your body *and* your mind.

It's never one or the other. The pain response is a complicated cycle of physical and psychological reactions. Physicians and psychologists describe it this way: there is an injury, imbalance, infection—something that triggers a neurological response in the body. The brain and nervous system send messages back and forth in an attempt to stop or reduce the pain or eliminate the source of it. Like an alert telling you to take your hand off the hot burner. But nerve cells can remain on high alert, even when the pain has changed, and the cells themselves change over time, sometimes remaining activated and in the pain state we refer to as chronic pain.

This alters how we behave, and that can once again contribute to our feelings of pain. For example, once we are injured or pain flares, we work to avoid it. We move differently, or not at all; we change what we do, and over time, some muscles and ligaments and nerves react differently altogether. In my case, the pain and stiffness and cartilage erosion in my joints make it difficult to move in certain ways, so my muscles and tendons around those joints have become tighter, restricting my movement even more and causing more pain when I try to walk, which of course makes me not want to move.

As our physical body is coping, our mind is sending out regular alerts that alter our moods and lead to frustration, anger, irritability. It chips away at our abilities to focus and concentrate, which causes more frustration. Finally, we may feel hopeless, disempowered, depressed, and that depression contributes to more physical pain. It's vicious. But here's the good news: while the physical conditions causing the pain can be difficult to manage, we can develop approaches that help ease the pain process in our brains. When we do that, our bodies experience some relief too.

Ouch!

While I live with some level of pain daily, there are three things that cause it to spike. Too much standing, or physical activity—fatigue—without proper rest. Stress. And weather changes. When my stress level is up and the barometric pressure is low, my body—and usually my mood—take a turn.

I can't control the weather, but I can put on a raincoat and weather the storm. And research indicates that we can do this by using our thoughts to protect us from a flood of physical pain.

Our beliefs influence how we experience pain. Often, when we are under stress, or dreading the pain before it's even occurred, we begin to ruminate and dwell. We start to worry about the pain we are going to feel, even before we hurt.

This adds to our stress, causing our muscles to tense up, which contributes to pain, prompting us to avoid healthy activity that could help us stay loose and more comfortable. And all these physical responses start in our brains.

This cycle is called pain catastrophizing. And it can limit the effectiveness of our pain medications and other interventions that can actually ease the hurt, says Beth Darnall, PhD, a pain specialist and the author of *The Opioid-Free Pain Relief Kit*.

As the pain increases, we can become sullen and sometimes depressed. We might replay negative thought patterns, like "My pain will never go away," or "There is nothing I can do, nothing helps." "My pain is only going to get worse."

We must disrupt these thought patterns to ease the pain. The pain catastrophizing mindset is marked by rigid thinking. It occurs when we view our pain experience in absolute terms. When we see it as constant, unrelenting, impossible to manage. None of those descriptions are accurate, because pain and our experience of it does change.

When we can stop ourselves from this kind of catastrophizing, take a breath, and catch ourselves in this negative thought pattern, we can pick a new one—one that will help us cope.

Reframing our experience of pain is, for me, the most powerful way to do this.

Consider these thoughts:

> I'm never going to feel better. There is nothing I can do.
> My pain will never go away.
> With all I've done today, I'm going to be miserable tomorrow.

Pretty defeating. Not even true. And, yet I've caught myself thinking all of them from time to time. When I change my perspective, my pain gets easier to bear. You can try it too.

INSTEAD OF SAYING, I'M NEVER GOING TO FEEL BETTER:
Try this: When I relax, my pain will ease.

INSTEAD OF, MY PAIN WILL NEVER GO AWAY:

Go with: My experience of pain changes all the time,
so I know I won't always feel like this.

INSTEAD OF, I'M GOING TO BE MISERABLE TOMORROW:

How about: Today was fun; tomorrow I'll rest and relax
so my body feels good.

Changing your thoughts alters the body's stress response, interrupting the pain cycle, and changing how we feel.

Another pain disruptor is to create a go-to relaxation response. This can even be part of your setback strategy, the Bounce-Back Kit we talked about in Chapter 17.

Darnall talks about the importance of identifying ten ways you can disrupt the pain catastrophizing process before you get stuck in it. She suggests that we start by writing down a few fun or calming activities we enjoy. I read, write my pages, golf, listen to podcasts, pet my cat, stretch, meditate. You might listen to music, paint, watch a show.

Make your list. Write it on an index card and carry it in your wallet or pocket, or put your list in a notes file on your phone, and when you feel yourself spiraling into pain and fear, pull it out and do one of those things. Disrupt the cycle before it takes hold, and you will plug the hole that can be an energy drain.

Mindfulness can also help. Try noticing your thoughts about what your body is experiencing and using all your senses to become present to what's happening within and around you. It's never just the pain. Sometimes, particularly when my fingers and wrists are hurting, I'll wash my hands slowly and mindfully under warm water, paying attention to the feel and sounds and the smell of the soap. The mindfulness practice helps me become present and shift my focus from the pain and interrupts any worries about pain in the future. The warm water and gentle movement ease the physical flare.

Or take some deep, mindful breaths. Try a deep breathing exercise, by slowly breathing in through your nose, to the count of five. Breathe deeply so that you can see your belly move out as your diaphragm expands. Hold for a count of two, then release through your mouth for a count of seven. Repeat at least five times.

Muscle relaxation can also help, by selectively tightening and holding your muscles for a five-count, then relaxing. Start at your feet and work up through your back, neck, and jaw, and you'll feel a release.

I've become more comfortable with my pain over the years because I have had a lot of practice putting these things in play. Some days are better than others. And each day requires awareness—paying attention to my thoughts, my body, my schedule—so I can adapt and change as needed to stay as comfortable and productive as possible.

Some days do require more energy to stay at baseline, for all of us really, pain or not. But, most days, I can do this well. While the pain never dissipates completely, I don't think about it all that much, and that perception keeps it from knocking me down like a bowling pin.

Despite the physical hurt, though, pain is also a major source of my fatigue, which I despise. This is perhaps the most difficult aspect of chronic illness for me, the tiredness. But it's also why I am so grateful for the moments when I do feel good, because that energy of appreciation carries me through the not-so-good ones.

If I'm going to be hurting and tired no matter what I do, I figure, I might as well go golfing, or out to dinner with friends, or watch a football game or sit outside on the deck. Because those fun things give me something better to focus on, and that helps me to plug the holes opened by the pain a little bit more. Be deliberate in what you give your attention to.

/ / /

I am so familiar with my pain experience that I really don't give it much attention. It's folded into my routine and I adjust as needed to accommodate it. I brush my teeth and golf and parent and cook. I have curly hair and brown eyes. I also live with some pain. It's part of my day, but not all I think about. Rarely a focal point. Until I go to the doctor.

There in the clinic, when I'm filling out those pre-check-in forms about symptoms and conditions, the doctors want to know what I feel like. What my pain level is. What hurts. What helps. And as I go through each question, my body begins to throb. When I look at the little emoji faces that show levels of discomfort from one to ten, I wind up feeling like I'm on fire. An eight. A ten, even! When only a few minutes earlier, just before I arrived, I was probably around four.

After filling out these forms, the pain has captured all of my attention. It's all I can see, feel, think about, talk about. It's crushing. Not the pain itself, but the thought of it. After the appointment, when I'm headed home, thinking about work and what to cook for dinner, it begins to lessen. By the end of the day, I'm back to my baseline. My middle zone.

Notice when your thoughts are focused on pain. Then use some of the ideas above to unwind the mental knots. This will help your body and mind relax. It will lower cortisol, and the other biochemicals that cause inflammation and other pain-igniting responses, and in the process, change the way we feel it.

And, for good measure, you can swear and it might just end the ache. I do. And it helps. I'll tell you why—in the next chapter.

CHAPTER 28

POWER WORDS

Last night at the dinner table—because we are classy like this—my husband, daughter, and I talked about our favorite cuss words.

Mine is easy. I prefer shit when I'm surprised, in pain, mad. When I drop the open package of straws and all 130 wind up on the kitchen floor looking like pick-up sticks—shit is the first place I go. When I twist my back reaching for the pot in the back? Shit.

On the rare occasion, my husband will say "damn." But he says it softly, as though he doesn't want his parents to hear. It's still thrilling for my high-school-aged daughter to cuss in front of her friends. But she won't say her favorite word in front of me. She spells it out, though. That makes me laugh.

For me, blurting out an occasional cuss word is such a release. It's a rush of energy and passion, and that often interrupts and supersedes all the other irritating messages playing through my head. It ends any discussion I'm having with a whiney internal voice. It's definitive. Like a 1950s father saying, "That's enough." I blurt out my cuss word. I move on.

Words—particularly the ones we say to ourselves—are powerful like this. They motivate us, help us process difficulty, lift us up, or tear us down.

Swearing, according to several studies, is actually an adaptive behavior. Richard Stephens, from Keele University in the United Kingdom, has found through several experiments that swearing is a way to communicate our strongest emotions, and can help us tolerate pain better. The right bad word motivates us, creates energy, underscores our feelings, ideas, concerns.

Researcher David Stillwell says, swearing indicates honesty. Often, people who swear are giving you their true opinion, their authentic response, rather than filtering their language to fit in.

And swearing can be a sign of happiness, comfort, and a way to create social bonds. Overused swear words and slurs picked to marginalize or denigrate others are a turn-off, however, revealing your beliefs in a way that can leave you isolated, and even unemployed. No good energy comes from using words to hurt or diminish others.

Cussing is a way to vent, a quiet exclamation, helps me during a round of golf, to release the frustration of a bad shot. This frees me up to focus on the next bad shot. But I'm not thinking of any of this when I knock my knee against the corner of the table or when I'm hanging with my girlfriends talking about mothering, marriage, menopause, and money. I'm just letting the words fly. And my friends do too.

It's no surprise, really, because according to another study, this one from Marist University, New York, cussing indicates a large vocabulary and verbal fluency. In other words, swearing is a sign of intelligence. Apparently, my friends are very, very smart.

Framing with Words

Polite words also have power, especially when we are trying to motivate ourselves toward healthier behaviors. And the way information is conveyed influences even more than the words themselves.

Psychologists call this the framing effect, and you see it at work all the time in commercials, politics, and activism.

Even my daughter uses this tactic when she wants sugary snacks from the store. She'll show me a package that says zero calories, no sugar added, or sugar-free in an attempt to get me to buy this "healthy" fruit snack. But no sugar added doesn't mean there isn't sugar in the product, only that no ingredients with sugar were added during processing.

Which hamburger do you buy, the kind that is 20 percent fat? Or 80 percent lean? Which would you pick, a jam with reduced sugar or one that has 25 percent less sugar? Same thing said differently.

The words we use impact our responses and outcomes. Even those quiet inner voices can inspire, motivate, excite, boost us up, or bring us down.

Can't/Don't

When it comes to how we talk to ourselves, "don't" has a more positive impact on our goals than the word "can't." Researchers Vanessa Patrick and Henrik Hagtvedt found that using the word "don't," as in, "I don't eat dessert," or "I don't eat after eight o'clock," can help people ignite their self-control and resist the kind of temptation that gets in the way of their goals.

In the study, 64 percent of those who said "I don't" instead of "I can't" when working toward healthier eating goals chose a healthier snack option when given a choice between a candy bar and a granola bar.

I get that. "I can't." feels limited and punishing. "I don't" feels like I'm in charge. "I won't" changes the implication again.

Carol Dweck, the psychologist known for her studies of growth mindset, has suggested we use the word yet, instead of no or I can't, when we are attempting to learn something new.

"I can't" or "It won't work," or "No" have clear negative connotations that, when used in certain contexts can thwart our progress, keeping us stuck in the status quo. Most of us can improve—at least a little—at anything we give effort to, so it's best that we not limit our energy by using language that does.

If we are working on an algebra problem, trying to flip an omelet or fix a software bug, we are more likely to work our way through the challenge when we use supportive, encouraging language.

Instead of saying "I can't cook," try, "I haven't learned how to flip the omelet yet." "Have you fixed the computer? Not yet."

"Yet" is growth-minded. It implies movement, progress. It sends a signal to our brain that we are working toward something. That we will figure it out, even though we haven't yet. That we have got this.

Could/Should

Should implies an obligation, necessity, probability, limited scope.

Could implies possibility, ideas, options. One is creative, one is expansive. Which would pique your energy and interest?

If you aren't sure which is more powerful, try it on your kid or partner.

Try saying this to your spouse or friend: "You should exercise more to become healthier."

Or "You could exercise more to feel healthier."

What about saying this to your teenager: "You should load the dishwasher right now." Or "You could load the dishwasher now."

Just writing them on the page feels different. One gets my mind churning with ideas. Should makes me feel heavy and burned-out. One more thing I gotta do. That's draining.

Want to recharge and fling yourself back into the flow of life? You should try changing the way you talk to yourself. Well, that sounds a tad bossy. But you could try talking to yourself differently—now that's an interesting idea and totally possible.

Olympic athletes who keep their self-talk positive despite pressure perform better. People who are constructive in their self-talk have been shown to be more effective leaders. This stuff changes our emotional energy, which alters our thoughts and behaviors.

Dropping the shoulds from my inner language took the heaviness off my daily schedule, and when I began considering the projects I could take on at work, rather than those I should be doing, I began to feel more energized and excited. When I opened up the way I used my language—the way I talked about my health, marriage, work—vitality flowed.

If You Could...

"If" is another word that can ignite creativity and innovation. Tim David talks about this in his book *Magic Words: The Science and Secrets Behind Seven Words That Motivate, Engage, and Influence*. And it feels better than "I don't know."

The word "if," David says, takes the pressure off. We all want to be right. We certainly don't want to appear dumb or wrong or inadequate, so if someone asks us a direct question, we are less likely to volunteer opinions or ideas if we are unsure of the correct answer.

But when encouraged to guess or imagine, we become more innovative. More willing to engage and participate in the discussion or process. More collaborative.

Try it. Answer these questions:

Do you know how many slices of pizza the average American eats every year?

Do you know what the safest car on the market is?

What is the only way to avoid layoffs when company revenues are down?

What do you most need to do to help your child succeed?

Do you know? Huh? No. I don't. And the threat of admitting that we don't know—especially in an office meeting or with a client—weighs heavily on people. It can stymie the conversation.

But what if I asked the questions this way: "If you could guess, how many slices of pizza do you think the average American eats per year?"

"If you were to pick the safest care on the market, what would it be?"

"If you could do anything, how would you avoid layoffs?"

"If you could do something to help your son be successful, what would you try?"

When we use our words this way, they encourage connection, conversation, collaboration, innovation. You are more likely to get good ideas from people who may not have offered them before, or at least open up possibilities that support your growth. We get energy from the words we use; pick powerful ones.

And BTW, the answer to the pizza question is forty-six slices. Americans eat forty-six slices of pizza, or forty pizzas a year, and twenty-three pounds of the saucy stuff, according to the pizza blog, Slice Life.

That's three billion total pizzas. Shit.

CHAPTER 29

TOMORROW WILL BE BETTER

Sometimes, sustaining energy, creating meaning, being present in your life, boils down to one thing: believing in something better.

Not like the earworm from Annie, "The Sun Will Come Out Tomorrow." This is not the Disney version. Who the heck knows what the wind will blow in? But here is what I do know: If the rain comes, I'll grab my jacket and work to stay dry.

I call this tomorrow optimism because, no matter how I feel right now, today, I can believe that tomorrow will be better—that the next moment can be brighter—and we can make that happen.

Scientists speculate that about a quarter of our optimism is a trait we are born with. The rest is a product of how we were raised, what we see, who we surround ourselves with, the habits and mindsets we draw on as adults. Optimism lingers on a spectrum, and most of us slide between pessimism and optimism throughout our lives, depending on what's going on.

And optimism is something we can choose. We can decide to believe that there are things each of us can do to make a positive difference. When we believe this way, we behave this way.

It calms me, knowing this. It's so hopeful. It's a big part of why I write these books. Because I want you to know this too. Your power. When we recognize that we can positively influence outcomes by how we think and behave, by the energy we bring, then we aren't as stressed.

Optimism isn't about positive thinking. It doesn't require you to suppress the bad feelings, gloss over the hard stuff. It isn't even about abandoning your pessimistic tendencies; we all have some. Pessimism can keep us practical and grounded. But optimism moves us to behave in a way that can help us navigate the tough stuff and create better outcomes.

When we do, we are healthier and have greater well-being. Optimism is an adaptive way of coping. It motivates us to try to improve the things we can, despite the turmoil. We don't have to sit in the madness and mess believing there is nothing we can do.

For example, I've never believed I could cure my rheumatoid arthritis, but I do believe there is plenty I can do to manage it well. Believing that has inspired me to take the steps to do it. Doesn't matter if I can control a chronic disease; I can choose to live well with it.

Acting optimistically creates tangible results. It helps us manage our moods, lowers our risk of depression, improves our heart health and immune function, enhances relationships, and adds to our longevity. Probably because a tendency toward optimism buffers against the stress that eats away at our health and well-being—mostly because optimism helps us cope, according to scores of studies. The optimistic tendency buffers us against the stress that eats away at our health and well-being. And get this—optimists even earn more money, according to some research.

Getting Optimisticky

There are several approaches you can take to lean into optimism—even if you are a skeptic. These are some that work for me.

Look for conscious gains. Psychiatrist Aparna Iyer recommends that we challenge ourselves to find more than one perspective. If you're constantly looking at the downside, switch it up. The more often we reframe things positively, the easier it becomes to do.

By cultivating an awareness of your thoughts like this, you can learn to consciously alter your thought processes and change the way your brain works, making it easier for you to see the positive side, according to researcher Richard Davidson. Mindfulness can help with this. When we notice our thoughts and feelings without judgment, we consciously shift from a state of stress and anxiety to a more relaxed state.

Savoring, taking thirty seconds to really enjoy the good feelings we experience, is another way.

As Davidson's research shows, over time, these kinds of optimistic thoughts and behaviors change our brain activity, altering the way we respond to negative situations. With practice, optimism becomes more automatic.

Limit the negative news. I don't watch television news. It freaks me out. Gets me yelling at the television and all my attention is focused on things that are falling apart. With around-the-clock media access, it's easy to get caught up in the things that aren't working. Make sure you are also getting a steady diet of puppy videos and cute baby pics and the helpers and the good guys. There are so many good people in the world. Look for them. I read the newspaper, now and still, to keep up-to-date and keep my energies balanced.

Keep it real. It's fine to lean toward the positive and believe that things will improve, but then you had better get to work making them happen. Optimism is an attitude and an action. Believe in something better and then start working toward those better-news-scenarios.

And yet, dang, sometimes life kicks my bum. It can be hard and painful and beautiful and perplexing all at the same moment. I can be grateful and mad. Happy and sad. We are layered and complex beings. But we are more than capable of holding it all because, as optimists, we know these upsets are temporary; life is fluid and dynamic and we can roll with it all. All the ups and downs.

Knowing this is such a relief on a hard workday, when nobody is buying my book, and my daughter just got through describing in detail why she is in love with some rapper who has a full-face tattoo, and the faucet is dripping.

Optimism won't fix the faucet, but if you believe it can be fixed, you'll find a way through this and every other challenge.

A friend's son, Kyler, was sitting downstairs, studying in the kitchen, when he noticed the "walls were raining." A problem with the upstairs plumbing destroyed carpet and ceilings and cupboards. Water had seeped into every nook and cranny, requiring a team of plumbers, restoration specialists, and contractors to work for eight weeks, rebuilding the interior from the studs up.

The damage cost thousands of dollars to repair. Everything had to be moved out of the house. Walls were torn out, carpet pulled. At the same time, everyone was working and attending school at home, online.

"I think I'm in denial a little bit," my friend Tonya told me, as a team of five plumbers and contractors wandered through. "It's just hard to process. It's overwhelming."

But within hours, with the clean-up underway, the silver linings began to show. "Well, our bathroom was old and worn and needed updating anyhow," she laughed. "So, guess now's a good time."

/ / /

Just like water, optimism can seep into everything—in the best ways—at the worst times. It's a habit we can develop. A better-making behavior we've got to choose. Then, we can turn to it when we need it.

Anyone can do it, even when you are feeling down and beaten and negative about the circumstances. After a really hard day at school or a disappointment that knocked the wind out of me, my mom would say, "Honey, just go to bed. Tomorrow will be better." And it was.

Believe in Something Better

If you believe there is nothing you can do, you will do nothing.

Beliefs are just high-powered thoughts—usually about ourselves or the way the world works. They are nothing more than ideas until we act on them. Our behaviors and actions make these ideas real.

If I choose to believe the best days are behind me, or that I can't make healthy changes, or that aging sucks, then I'm more likely to behave in ways that support those beliefs.

Believe in something better, and you create better things.

Doesn't mean the house won't flood. It just means that when it does, you'll wade through the water, pour yourself a glass of wine, and start pulling carpet.

Optimistic behavior allows for the possibility of something even just a teeny bit better to arrive. This is tomorrow optimism. It isn't foo-foo optimism. It's real and grounded and practical. Life is in the doing, and optimism is the doing. You've got to behave as if what you are doing will get you where you want to go. The focus is on now.

Life is dynamic, fluid. It's an energy exchange. When we move with it, we shape that energy in a way that raises us up.

You get it, right? There is energy in believing that we can influence positive outcomes. That we are capable of making this moment a little bit better—no matter how crappy it is—and when we get up to do that, better things happen.

A Positive Charge

How can you harness these ideas and beliefs to recharge? What gets you excited? What turns you on to life? What do you want to try? How can you contribute? Put it on your to-do list for tomorrow. Do you want to create? Become healthier? Spend more time with family? Hike in a new locale? Start a routine of afternoon naps or early-morning meditations?

Now choose an action from your to-do list that you believe is worth doing. And start the doing. You might feel nervous or unsure. Maybe excited, too. Optimism builds when we have things we are looking forward to. This is how we up our energy.

We think about what moves us. Consider what you want to do or improve or change. Reflect on how it could enhance your energy. Maybe even help others. Decide it's a worthy effort. Go toward that. And that, right there, is optimistic action. It's what drives us forward into something better. Optimism is the movement between ideas and action.

This does more than fill our tank with energy. It makes us unstoppable even when it feels as though all the world is conspiring to hold us back.

CHAPTER 30
ALL THE FEELS

You know that feeling you get when you are cuddled up with a good book in front of a hot fire on a stormy day—with nowhere to go? It's called—er, what do you call it?

The Danish call it hygge (*hyoo·guh*), but until 2017, when the Oxford English Dictionary added it to their pages, it wasn't an official word in the English lexicon. We didn't have a word for that comfy, cozy, relaxed, secure feeling.

Now we do. And the word hygge comes loaded with meaning. It's a noun, verb, and adjective, and, though definitions differ depending on who you talk to—some include mentions of blankets and candlelight—most agree that hygge is that intangible sense of well-being and comfort.

A slew of other words jittered through my mind last night when my fourteen-year-old told me of her plan to tattoo the inside of her wrist with a sewing needle and the ink of a ballpoint pen. Revolted. Interested. Amazed.

When I failed to endorse her artistic vision (air quotes), she became furious. Or angry? Maybe it was frustrated. It was clear that she was very emotional.

These emotions occur in the limbic system of our brains. When triggered by an event or other stimuli, our limbic system activates creating a biological reaction.

Say you have an hour left before a big project deadline at work, and the computer is acting glitchy and you wind up losing part of the document that's due. Then your supervisor piles on by asking that another element be added in. In your frustration, you might cry, or start to tremble, get a headache, feel your heart beat faster.

That physical response is emotion. The words you use to describe those emotions—like overwhelm, anger, stress, scared—are feelings.

When your shoulders tighten and your heart beats faster because of the pressure at work, you are having an emotional response to those circumstances. Events and thoughts triggered a physiological shift.

The First Ninety Seconds

Years ago, a psychologist explained how circumstances—unkind words, someone cutting us off on the freeway, a betrayal or hurt—triggers a neurochemical response that surges through our bodies, instantly changing how we feel and think.

From the initial trigger, which causes the automatic chemical release in our brains and bodies, to the moment those chemicals have pulsed through our bloodstream, ninety seconds elapse.

Yet we can feel bad for days. If the upset persists, it's often because our thoughts are replaying the initial trigger and first emotional response. If we just stay mindful during those first ninety seconds, just sit in and observe it, the rush of emotion and feeling will change. That fast. We don't have to be encumbered by it. It doesn't have to stick to us.

///

I once visited a castle in Tuscany. My friend, another therapist (I love therapists), and I climbed the narrow stone stairs to the wide flat roof, where we could look at the rolling hills and the valley below. As I came nearer to the edge, my legs felt doughy, I trembled, my throat tightened. Then my friend asked me something I've thought about and repeated ever since. "Are you anxious or excited?"

The two feel very similar in our bodies, but the way we define and describe the physical sensations changes how we feel and respond to our circumstances. Our feelings are influenced by our interpretation, thoughts, beliefs, memories, and experiences. Their power is in the meaning we give them and the words we choose to explain them.

Defining the Feeling

We all experience several core emotions. Anger and sadness. Happiness and fear, disgust, surprise, embarrassment, and nuances and shades of each. These emotions are common, and our bodies are biologically wired to respond. Our blood pressure rises, our breathing changes, our heartbeats adapt, our muscles fire; we might feel hot or flush, tense or relaxed. Our eyes might become wider.

But you might describe these sensations as exhilarating when I could call them fear—particularly if I'm standing at the edge of a drop-off.

Happiness, the emotion, might be expressed through a smile or laugh. Your body warms, muscles relax, and the feeling you hold may be that everything is good, all is right with the world, and life can't get any better. You might remember a great day at the beach with your dad, or the day you got your first car. The emotion floods you with neurotransmitters like dopamine and serotonin. The feeling is a good one, and it's good for our well-being. Positive emotion is a powerful energy booster.

Yet, when we are experiencing an uncomfortable emotion and describe it as a feeling like stress, fear, or anger, we'll also experience higher levels of cortisol or adrenaline surging through our bodies. Sustained levels of cortisol can lead to inflammation, high blood pressure, reduced immune function, and chronic illness.

While the terms emotions and feelings are often used interchangeably, when we broaden our understanding of our emotional reactions and feelings, we can manage them more effectively.

The fear you experience while waiting for biopsy results is probably very different from the fear you feel if you encounter a garter snake in the garden. The happiness we feel on our wedding day is often a different degree of happiness than what we experience when we get a new pair of shoes.

When we get specific about what it is we are feeling, we can manage better. Instead of seeing everything as a threat, we can change our experience with the words we choose to describe it. To do this, we've got to develop a larger emotional vocabulary.

We don't want to sum up our peak experiences with the same word we use to describe lunch at a drive-thru: good. People are more layered than nice. Some movies are bad. Cancer is bad. But to me, those two don't carry the same weight. We love those shoes and tater tots. We love our child, too. But it's not the same, is it? Not even close. Tater tots for the win.

A limited emotional vocabulary, then, limits our lives. We miss out on the nuances and the feelings and textures and colors of our experiences and the meaning and energy within them.

Use Your Words

Our days take on the energy of the feelings we express, and our feelings often feel bigger and heavier the longer we stay with them. If we don't take time to understand what it is we are feeling and what is behind the mad or the sad (like frustration, disappointment, or boredom), our feelings tend to overpower us.

This is what happened when I was feeling the midlife slump that prompted this book. I described every day with the same single sentence, "Good, but tired."

No wonder I felt blasé. Of course, I felt fatigued. I eliminated a range of possibilities and experiences by limiting the way I described my feelings. Processed every feeling the same way. Using the same words to describe each day kept me stuck in the same low-energy feeling.

When I became more specific about my feelings, my days began to change too. But I had to learn some new words. So, like every enlightened soul everywhere, I Googled.

The Emotional Pie

To change how we experience our emotions and feelings, we have to be able to identify them. I had a pretty narrow emotional vocabulary before I started. A few of my favorite feelings were overwhelmed, tired, busy, curious, interested, good, happy. I used them to describe everything.

Then I found variations of the Plutchik Wheel of Emotions, and I felt astonished, eager, surprised, and inquisitive.

Psychologist Robert Plutchik believed we have a small number of basic or primary emotions, like anger, sadness, and happiness, and a range of others that evolve from those, differing by degree and intensity.

When we label those unique feelings, we cope with them better, according to a study from the University of California, Los Angeles. Verbalizing them makes our sadness and anger less intense.

Understanding the specific underlying feeling illuminates the reasons behind our joy or upset, helping us to manage our anger or hurt and relish our happiness.

Hurt is a very different feeling from anger, for example. Yet we often get mixed up between the two, flashing to anger instead of feeling vulnerable or open about why we are hurting. When we come clean with the accurate label, we can spend our energy transforming the conditions that contribute to the pain, rather than simply trying to cope with them.

Finding the specific words to match my feelings became a practice in itself that moved me from a state of dissatisfaction to one of engagement. I got curious. Boom! There is energy there. I started paying attention to my emotions—the physical sensations in my body—and the words I used to describe them.

Instead of repeating that I was tired at the end of the day, I began slinging around words like calm, curious, isolated, lonely, dismayed, content, bored. It's become one of my many (and annoying, according to the teen) quirks to find a more precise word to describe my feelings.

'Course I do need help with the emotional vocab, so I printed out a colorful emotion wheel and stuck it to the refrigerator with a dragonfly magnet. Now, whenever someone leaves dirty dishes in the sink or puts an empty milk jug back in the fridge, I have exactly the right word to describe my feelings.

Curate the energy of your emotions. Develop a more complex emotional vocabulary and some emotional intelligence so the feelings add, teach, and bolster your energy, helping you recharge rather than be tossed in the froth of a sea of emotions.

CHAPTER 31

PACING

I'm reading more these days.

Not just a few minutes at bedtime when my body readies for sleep, but also after work and sometimes on Saturday mornings before others are up.

I'm also spending more time outside. And cooking. Jeez Louise, am I cooking. Playing the ukulele. And having deeper, more interesting conversations with my husband, and petting the dog. Playing cards with my kid. It's slower, now, a little more settled here. It's about pacing.

In the early days, the pandemic played out like a perpetual snow day, without the joy. Or the snow. But life got quiet and still. There was little traffic on the road behind our house. People stayed in. Life hushed.

It wasn't lazy, just slower, because we didn't have anywhere to go. I was trying to figure out remote schooling with my daughter, sharing an office with my husband. We learned to buy groceries online—toilet paper, check, wipes, check—and how to video-conference with my folks. But there were no early trips to the gym, no errands or appointments to run, no meals out or soccer games or back-to-school nights. No commutes.

So, despite my heartache as the pandemic spread, most of my energy was going to the things that filled me up—like being home, listening to music with my daughter, eating dinner together. My energy wasn't being sucked out by endless errands or school commutes or meetings that stripped me down and wore me out. The change of pace prompted me to start doing more of the little things in life that help me feel good, calm, grounded. Appreciative, aware, grateful.

Often in life, I've felt this pull between taking time for the things that help me restore, feel good and healthy, and the things I think I should be doing. Now, I know this comes down to self-care. Doing the things that contribute to my well-being ignites the kind of calm energy I need to take care of the others and get stuff done. But even while I'd been doing some "me-things" before, there was always some pressure, a sense that I should be doing something else. Everything felt hurried, time was compressed.

When life was slowed by circumstance, I realized that, to recharge at any point, we need to regulate our pace. To stay well and good and to maintain the relationships we treasure, we've got to reduce our schedules. Eliminate the things that drain us without replenishment. To take one thing at a time. To become fine with missing out instead of living with the fear of it. We feel burned-out and frazzled when our energy is scattered. To recharge, we've got to establish a pace that supports us.

I'm focused on now. One thing at a time. One singular event, topic, conversation, moment. I'm working to engage in that without watching the clock. I avoid my email when I'm writing a story. I do not look at my phone while golfing. When I'm petting the dog, I am petting the dog. She loves this, all this attention. Then I'm done with that and I do the next thing. There is a calm kind of comfort in this. A kind of happiness that comes when you go all in. Give yourself to that moment instead of worrying about the next one.

Go slow and steady. Allow the energy of those moments to fill you up, rather than leave you frazzled.

A study from the University of Zurich and Radboud University in the Netherlands, led by motivational psychologist Katharina Bernecker, explains that happiness and well-being evolve out of our capacity to savor the simple pleasures without being bombarded by thoughts of the other things we should be doing.

Pursuing goals, creating habits that support our values and desires—such as eating healthier foods to achieve weight loss—and cultivating the self-control needed to accomplish our long-term goals leaves us feeling happier and more satisfied.

Two Speeds

But Bernecker's research indicates both periods of striving and of settling are essential to living with vibrancy. After spending years feeling frantic and impatient, my mind spinning from one idea into the next, I've stopped doing that. Mostly. There is more space between the lines of my to-do list. Not every moment is filled. I want to leave time to read in the morning, to drink coffee on the back deck. To have a long lunch with my daughter when she's on break. To work without interruption. To no longer feel the pressure to do it all. And in these open spaces, energy percolates and bubbles.

This focus on pacing has helped me slow my roll in a way that makes me better at the things I decide to do, and it's all more fun.

In the study, Bernecker says, "The pursuit of hedonic and long-term goals needn't conflict with one another. Our research shows that both are important and can complement each other in achieving well-being and good health."

To do it, though, we can't let our thoughts crash in, crowding out the good feelings, keeping us from savoring the moment.

Watch your pace. Make time to strive and work and build and create. Make time to rest, restore, savor, notice. Honor your downtime, the simple pleasures, as something essential to your success, in the same way you honor your job, family responsibilities, household needs.

Talk back to the inner critic who tells you to get up and go, rather than take it slow.

Protect time on a Saturday afternoon to do whatever you like. Or use the mini-breaks throughout your day to relax, read a few pages in a book, or savor a good meal, water the plants, hit the trails for a hike, knit, or paint, or stretch, pet the cat, or mindfully listen to music by your favorite band.

It's not about replacing your drive for the more demanding tasks with slower simpler, pleasures, but stitching together a more holistic life. One that includes both, a contrast of energies: one that allows your mind, spirit, body to recharge, and the other to release.

In the end, you honor your life by enjoying it.

CHAPTER 32

HAPPY-HOUR THERAPY

When my friend's marriage ended, we talked about it in the wooden booth at the pub down the street. We've debated medical treatments, talked through parenting dilemmas, complained about financial stresses, marriage challenges, workplace politics, politics politics. We've discussed endings and beginnings, over nice long dinners and back-deck gatherings, for years now. What hasn't varied is the nourishment I get from this kind of connection.

Social connection is like that. We just do better when we come together. It isn't the number of friends that matter, it's the quality of connection. Research by Steve Cole, the head of the Social Genomics Core Laboratory at the University of California, Los Angeles, shows that a lack of social connections carries a higher health risk than obesity and smoking.

With a strong social group, you are also apt to live longer. We do better as part of a tribe. Social connection strengthens our immune system, lowers inflammation, lowers our risks for anxiety and depression, and breeds better cooperation and relationships.

This is why I happy-hour. Though I'm an introvert, happiest at my desk or behind a book, I feel lost when I haven't connected with those I hold close. I don't always notice it in the beginning—but I'm more restless, edgy. I feel uprooted, insecure. I'm just not as good without my friends.

It's harder to get together now. Kids' schedules, job demands, people living in different cities, and aging parents tug at our time and attention now. These things all compete for our energy. Sometimes I don't feel like I have enough left for an evening visit. But I drag on my jeans, paw through the drawer for a clean shirt, and I go. And even before I've pulled into the driveway at the end of the evening, I'm shaping the text in my head.

"Thanks, you guys. So good to see you. I always feel so much better after a visit. I love you."

I don't go out often. I'm no longer the girl who says, "I'll give you a call" when we run into each other at the grocery store, because I know myself better now and I know I won't do it. Not anymore.

I'm discerning, not because I don't care about the others, but because I've learned to hold my energy close, so I have enough to nourish the ones who also nourish me.

Relationships adapt, or they die. My friends and I have gone from making gingerbread houses when the kids were little to dressing for dinner and a show. Early drinks on a summer evening on the back deck and Zoom calls in sweats. Monthly dinners at a pub. Even visits on a cold, wet soccer field. Not saying I loved it. But I love them.

Studies show the deepest connection occurs when we can look each other in the eyes—even digitally—and hear the changes in tone or voice and see smiles and gestures. And if there is someone you love, tell them. Share that energy, nourish those souls and your own. This is how we recycle the good energy we get from being together. This recharges all of us.

Coming Close

Friendships and meaningful connections require us all to invest. To be brave and put ourselves out there, to risk discomfort, and fatigue, rejection even, to give our energy in the hopes of creating a nurturing sustainable connection.

Only when we move close to each other, after some time and patience, do we develop the intimacy we crave. The intimacy and connection that comes when we feel truly known and accepted just as we are.

The people whom I share this with have impacted everything in my life. Science shows that we are deeply influenced by our friends and romantic partners. The right ones can make you better.

If you are married to or hang out with someone who is a healthy eater, you're likely to eat healthier. Friends who are kind, funny, open, and driven are likely to elicit those qualities in you.

Self-control tough for you? Hang with people who have a high degree of it and you'll do better, according to a study[1] published in *Psychological Science*. You are more likely to achieve your goals when you have friends who are go-getters. Those friends who are strong-willed (yep, I know a little something about strong-willed friends) will inspire you to keep going. When I say my friends make me better, I'm not kidding. They raise me up.

---

1 www.psychologicalscience.org/index.php/news/releases/low-on-self-control-surrounding-yourself-with-strong-willed-friends-may-help.html

You Are Not a Lonesome Loser

If you're not feeling close ties right now, you are not alone—even if it seems as though you are. More than a quarter of all Americans say they feel lonely, and that number is growing so rapidly that loneliness is now considered a public health crisis.

As more of us work from home and so much of our communication is happening via text or teleconference, we are missing the in-person collaboration and eye contact that is one of our most primal, tribal needs. Gone are the handshakes and hugs, and other appropriate physical touches, that are essential to our well-being.

Loneliness makes it harder to weather the stresses of life and raises our risk of illness and depression. If you feel nervous about getting out there and developing relationships, know this: it's a lot more uncomfortable and depleting over the long haul to live in this place of loneliness. It wears on us.

Breach it by creating opportunities to meet others. Set up a Zoom call with someone you haven't talked to in years. Join a club or association focused on your interests, whether it be books or mountain climbing or gold panning, and chances are you'll meet others who share an interest in the things you care about. That's an easy way to begin a conversation. Or pick up a sport, like golf, or tennis, where you are paired up to play with others. You'll have a fun afternoon even if you don't make a lasting friendship.

Wade into the social pool by doing things you enjoy, and you'll most likely meet people you enjoy. If you are feeling low and lonely, it isn't because you are unlikable. It's because you aren't out there. Loneliness is a feeling, not a character trait or flaw. And it's one feeling you can change.

It also helps if you keep your head up in the world, extend yourself, make eye contact, volunteer for causes you believe in, show interest in others without expecting anything in return. Smile at people you pass on the sidewalk. Say "hey." Help a neighbor. That connection will raise your energy.

I made new friends when I joined a community group working to feed hungry kids. I met Tonya, my friend of the flooded house and one of my BFFs, when I took my daughter to a kid's birthday party. Tonya was standing around. I was standing around. We started chatting. I'm awkward at small talk, but she was open and friendly, so I go through it. We've been friends for years.

Of course, some friendships will drop away. We'll grow into others. Appreciate the gifts and let them expand or end naturally, as they do. But, when you find a few that fit, a few you can show up for, no lipstick required, bring your best.

Be true. Authentic. Let people know when you are thinking of them. Respond to their texts. Help in the way they need to be helped. Apologize when you are a doofus and get to a happy hour every few months or more. Those relationships will inspire and elevate you. They will make you better.

Even for an introvert like me, who needs some quiet time to recoup, there is an energy I get from my closest friends. They lift me up. And they sustain me during the hard times.

These are the people I want to drink beer with. That has always been my gauge. There are lots of people whom I care for, but only a few I'd spend an hour with, drinking beer. These people provide the laughs, and the support, the wisdom and the joy, all for the price of an amber ale.

Real Therapy

Happy hours with friends are affordable therapy, but real therapy, like the kind with a licensed professional, is another one of my favorite recharging practices. First off, a therapist's office is so calm and quiet. Nobody is ever pounding on the bathroom door for you to let them in so they can borrow (steal) the tweezers.

I dip in and out of professional therapy every couple of years. More often when I'm feeling stressed, confused, or unsettled. I go to vent, to understand, to become more compassionate, to learn about myself, and how to play well with others.

And I get an hour to work through things. Win-win. Therapy with a licensed professional helps you make sense of the things you are struggling with so you can adapt and move through these roadblocks rather than staying in the stagnant energy of them.

A therapist is like a physician for the mind and spirit. Often your friends can make a referral, or you can find licensed professionals listed by specialty on various websites. The right counselor will be wise, practical, honest, comforting, transparent about their credential and billing process. They will take time to listen, and sometimes challenge you, pushing you toward new thought patterns and ideas. They will not be judgmental or preachy. This is another kind of connection. Not a friend, but an ally. We all need allies.

When we surround ourselves with the right people, a professional pit crew of doctors and therapists and hairstylists and sommeliers, the families we are born to and the people we choose, our energy inflates. The company we keep raises us up.

Cultivate your tribe. Care for those who inspire you. Those who teach and support and challenge you. Care for those who know you completely and love you anyhow. Care for those who cast their light onto you, so you become brighter when you are in their presence. Be this light for them too. Give some energy to developing these ties, and you will be nourished even while you nourish others. This is a way to plug back into the energy we've lost. This is the way to elevate our lives. To ramp up our energy and enjoy our lives always.

CHAPTER 33

GOOD ENOUGH

"Mom, look. I gave myself bangs at three in the morning."

I open my eyes. Trying to focus. Jagged fringe of hair across her forehead.

"Good one," I say.

"Jeez Louise," I think.

Still, I offer up a fist bump, grab a cuppa in the kitchen, and carry it to work in the home office. I look for the file I'd almost finished the day before. Hmmm. Isn't showing up. Must be in another folder. Nope, not there, must be. Shit. Gone. The revisions I spent hours on didn't save. No history to restore. I try and I try to recover it. I miss a client call trying. Then, I spill the coffee on my desk.

The entire morning felt about as ragged as those middle-of-the-night bangs. The lost file, missed client call, spilled coffee, are little setbacks that feel big and hard when they come all at once. But then we go again. It was a mess of a morning, but I kept showing up and giving the best I had right then.

Some days are like this, right? Some moments seem hard, askew, fractured. But all we need to do is keep showing up. Consistent effort over time is our most powerful strategy.

The effort might feel uneven. Desperate, even. Sometimes we'll give our all and find our all sucks. Maybe it only amounts to 47 percent and that's after you got your real pants on and combed your hair. Sometimes our 100 percent will be sunny and smooth and flowy, and we'll be in the zone, spinning everything to gold.

While the golden days feel better, what matters most is having the day. Any day at all. And when we get that gift, we need to show up, give it our best, and be joyful about being just good enough. Give what you have. It counts.

You have my permission to be good enough. You don't have to be the best or perfect or shiny or polished. When you lose the file, yell at your kid, spill the coffee, forget the milk, miss the deadline, when you wear the hoodie with a hole in the sleeve, or track mud in the house without realizing, it's not because you are bad or wrong or dumb. It's just because. Don't give energy to second-guessing. Be the best you have right now. It's enough. You are just right.

Some days this kind of good looks very mediocre. Mediocre is fine. Jeez Louise, some days I am so grateful for mediocre. I don't know why it ever became a liability. If you can be worn and tarnished, a little messy and bruised, and totally, completely, utterly human, you are doing just fine. Show up. Do your thing. It's enough.

Consistent effort over time—give the best you have right then. Show up tomorrow and give your best again. That counts. You count. The energy you bring matters. Be good. Enough.

CHAPTER 34

WISHING YOU WELL

The woman in the white Subaru turned across two lanes of traffic, cutting me off at the merge. She didn't even look at me. Maybe she didn't see me, I don't know. I pulled hard to the right, disappearing into a cloud of dust on the shoulder. I avoided the collision. She kept right on going.

The muscles around my jaw and up into the corners of my eyes were stretched tight. A fireball of stress and fear and anger. I yelled. Cussed. Hit the steering wheel.

I wanted this stranger in the Subaru to feel afraid too. Just like me. To recognize her recklessness. To be punished in some way. To apologize. I wanted to flip her off.

But I took a deep breath, and another. Let my heartbeat settle. Wrestled a moment with my feelings. Then, I chose compassion.

She must be distracted, stressed, I thought. She wasn't out to get me, just needed to get where she was going. I'm glad nobody was hurt. It was a mistake, nothing more. And I've made a couple of those in my life.

I gave her the benefit of the doubt. Silently, I wished her well. Extended compassion.

I'd like to tell you I did this because I'm an awesome and enlightened person. Yeah. I'd also like to tell you that I weigh a healthy 120 and have never yelled at my sweet cherub child or eaten Cheetos for dinner. But no. There is no special bright light shining down on me. I don't walk around with a blissful smile on my face. Most days, I'm just happy if I get a shower and get my teen to talk to me during dinner.

I write books like this one because these are the things I'm learning too. These are the things I'm working on, the kind of energy I want to bring. And what I've learned is that hanging on to anger and stress and hostility and fear doesn't leave me feeling good.

Sure, I bitched for a few minutes, felt the energy of adrenaline and fear and anger shoot through the nooks and crannies of my body. Then, I just felt bad and shaky and scared. I felt icky.

There is a time for focused, managed anger—if you are deliberate and aware, you can use it to motivate. Anger toward racial injustice, for example, can ignite protests, legislation, change. Anger toward a doctor you feel isn't taking you seriously might prompt you to find better care. But feeling hostile toward the Subaru stranger did nothing but leave me tired. There was no change to effect here, so the energy stirred and stuck within my body. I felt weaker because of it.

Energy builds from compassion. Compassion is the act of recognizing or understanding the pain or discomfort of another and wanting to do something to help alleviate their suffering. This is different from empathy, which is about noticing and recognizing the pain of others. Compassion drives you to ease it. It's active. A decision you make. And it requires some emotional courage, because to help someone who is hurting, or who has hurt you, requires you to take a look at your own story, your own pain. And then offer relief, even to those who appear to deserve it the least.

But when we practice compassion, it changes our brains and gives us more control over our thoughts, and our lives, according to Paul Gilbert, PhD, Professor of Clinical Psychology at the University of Derby, and others who study the quality.

Feeling recharged is about pulling in the energy that elevates us. Kindness does that. Compassion does that. It's not about faking it. It's doesn't require that you suppress your bad feelings. It does require you to recognize that everyone makes mistakes, everyone feels hurt and anger and fear, and then it gives us the option to choose something better for ourselves and for others. Compassion is good for all of us.

Not About You

One way to edge into this kind of compassion is to recognize that most people aren't out to get you. When they do bad things or act inappropriately, that's about them, not us. We don't have to take that in. Their bad behavior doesn't have to influence ours. Most people are just doing what they do. Coping with what they know. Wrestling with their own backgrounds and beliefs. Falling back into their own default pattern based on their backstory.

You don't need to hang out with them. Don't need to take in that energy or stay close to their bad behavior. But they aren't picking on us, either. It is not about us.

The Subaru didn't try to take *me* out, I just happened to be there when she pulled across the lanes. The anger didn't belong to me. The fear did. The concern did. But the anger, no. I let it go and cultivated compassion. Not because I'm benevolent, but because it works better.

With compassion, you recognize the pain or discomfort experienced by others and you give them a break. You do something to try to relieve the pain. You edge toward the understanding that they are worried and frustrated. That perhaps something buried in their background is a trigger causing them to lash out, feel insecure, angry, hostile. Instead of meeting that hostility, you can go with something even higher.

Compassion for me acts as a lightning rod. I can be hit by this volatile energy—anger or disregard—and feel my own energy pique like a shard of glass. But I don't need to act on that irritation. Instead, I can transform it into a more compassionate peace. On my best day, this allows me to look at others and situations and challenges without judgment, but with understanding. The knowledge that we all hurt, and love, and desire. We are all humans just doing what we do. Sometimes what comes into our lives feels good, sometimes it doesn't. But I can always choose compassion.

Giving a Break

In the end, we'll be better off. Wishing others well layers on our own happiness, according to Iowa State University psychologists. It isn't what we do for ourselves that increases happiness, but what we offer others that matters most.

To test that theory, researchers recruited college students to walk around a building for twelve minutes.

During that time, one group of students was asked to look at people and offer loving-kindness—an approach often used in meditation that has you sincerely and silently wishing others happiness, comfort, ease, protection. Another group of students was directed to look at others and compare how much better off they were than the people they passed.

Those who offered up thoughts of kindness felt happier, more connected, empathetic[2], and less anxious[3], according to researcher Douglas Gentile.

The other group, the ones who compared themselves to others, didn't fare as well. They felt less empathetic, less caring, and less connected, according to the study. Comparison often makes us feel more competitive and isolated. Two things that increase our stress and diminish our energy.[4]

I think that's what happened there on the freeway. In my fear[5] over the near-miss accident, and then the anger[6] at being cut off, I started to make some comparisons. I felt angry that I'd been disrespected because I deserved more. My thoughts had this whole "who-does-she-think-she-is" tone.

It took me a minute, but then I recognized that the other driver isn't all that different from me. She was in a hurry too. She wants to stay safe too. With this understanding, I found it easier to extend compassion by silently sending her peace. I wished her well, safe travels. I gave thanks that I was safe too. This felt better. The upset didn't cling. You know, giving her the benefit of the doubt gave me a break, too.

It's harder to get unstuck when you are diagnosing all the bad in the world. There is plenty, lots of conflict, people doing awful

---

2 www.psychologytoday.com/us/basics/empathy
3 www.psychologytoday.com/us/basics/anxiety
4 www.psychologytoday.com/us/basics/stress
5 www.psychologytoday.com/us/basics/fear
6 www.psychologytoday.com/us/basics/anger

things. It's easy to get mired in the doldrums, where I did spend some serious time in my phase of malaise.

In the harder moments, when I was feeling angry or unraveled, unappreciated, or left out, I turned to a loving-kindness meditation, to expand the energy in my own life by extending peace to others. To be frank, it mellowed me out big time.

Loving-Kindness Meditation

I often use my own version of a loving-kindness meditation as part of my morning ritual because it helps me get grounded while recognizing the interconnectedness of us all. There are many versions of this meditation. And you can adapt it in your own way too. It's all about extending love and kindness, peace and compassion, to others. Understanding that everyone wants to feel safe like me. Happy, like me. Protected, like me. Aren't those things we all want?

Ready to try your own loving-kindness meditation? Here's how to do it.

Start by sitting comfortably with your feet flat on the floor and your spine straight. Close your eyes. Relax.

Take a deep breath in. And breathe out.

Receive Loving-Kindness

Keep your eyes closed and think of a person who loves you. It could be someone from the past or the present; someone still in life or who has passed; it could be a parent or spouse. Friend. Spiritual teacher or guide. Imagine that person standing on your right side, sending you their love. That person is sending you wishes for your safety, for your well-being and happiness. Feel the warm wishes and love coming from that person toward you.

Now imagine that you are surrounded on all sides by all the people who love you and have loved you. Picture all of your friends and loved ones surrounding you. Take it in. They want you to be happy and well. They want you to feel loved.

Sending Loving-Kindness

Now bring your awareness back to an individual. Might be a loved one, someone you are in conflict with, or even someone you have neutral feelings about. You are simply extending loving-kindness energy to this person. Remembering that this person wants to feel safe and loved and protected just like you.

Holding this person in mind, repeat the following phrases, silently:

> May you live with ease.
>
> May you feel safe and protected.
>
> May you be happy.
>
> May you be comfortable and free from pain.
>
> May your life be filled with happiness, health, and well-being.

You can also take a different approach to this meditation and focus on the interconnectedness with this Just Like Me Meditation.

While sitting quietly, bring a person to mind and repeat the following phrases.

This person has a body and a mind, just like me.

This person has feelings, thoughts, and emotions, just like me.

This person has during his or her life experienced physical and emotional pain and suffering, just like me.

This person has at some point been sad, just like me.

This person has been disappointed in life, just like me.

This person has sometimes been angry, just like me.

This person has been hurt by others, just like me.

This person has felt unworthy or inadequate at times, just like me.

This person wishes to be happy, just like me.

This person wishes to be safe, strong, and healthy, just like me.

This person wishes to be loved, just like me.

This person is learning about life, just like me.

May this person be filled with love, health, well-being, and happiness, just like me.

Don't worry about repeating the phrases just right. There are a lot of versions. You can even develop your own. The one I repeat is simple and short, so I can remember it. Usually, I extend loving-kindness to a specific individual, then to all people, and myself by saying:

May you live with comfort and ease.

May you feel safe and protected.

May you be happy.

May you be healthy.

May you feel loved and loving.

If I'm struggling or hurting or stressed, I'll start my morning with a loving-kindness meditation focusing my attention inward at first, then extending it out to others, sometimes even complete strangers, like those who lost their homes to wildfires or someone dealing with a difficult diagnosis. Other times it will be for a friend who is hurting, or even someone I feel conflicted about. This raises my energy too.

When you are done with the meditation, sit quietly for a minute longer. Take a deep breath in. Breathe out. Open your eyes.

This process of wishing others well, of sending love, leaves me calmer. I feel more connected and forgiving when I remember that, like me, all people want to feel safe and protected, healthy, and happy. This meditation allows us to recognize our humanity, the interconnectedness of us all.

Sending this out into a troubled world just feels better than adding to the pain. I have limited energy. I just don't have enough to be stuck in the hurt. I'm betting you don't either. This helps me remember that. It's a gentle way to recharge.

CHAPTER 35

RAISE IT UP

So, what now?

That's what I asked myself three years ago. And I began making the notes, trying things out, adopting habits and practices that I could use to recharge my mind, body, spirit. My life. Those are the things I shared with you here.

Those are the things I still practice today. I did lose weight. Still drinking smoothies. My writing work is developing in a fun and exciting way. I am healthier than I was, and that's helped me manage my pain and delay joint replacement surgery. But I'm getting closer to it now. I think I'm ready. I did start golfing again. Reading more. I'm better about pacing myself. Taking time to nourish my energy before I feel exhausted, depleted. I make time to create, explore, sleep, move.

I signed the agreement to write *You, Recharged* on a Friday, twelve hours before we were notified that my daughter, like so many other students, would finish out her year remotely. We celebrated her eighth-grade graduation with a car parade, celebrated our birthdays on Zoom, waited for text updates about my father's surgery. No visitors allowed. He is fine.

We are all fine. We've had ups and downs, but energy is like that, right? It fluctuates. Transfers. Transforms. But it won't dim if we don't let it. We know, now, how to keep our spark.

We are resilient. All of us. Strong, agile. Knowing this, believing this about yourself, cultivates that good energy And what I have learned is that, when we continue to nourish and cultivate our vitality, we have more energy to circulate in the world. Our good energy expands, transforms, elevates everything else. Even now. Especially now.

Circumstances don't diminish high energy. They transform it. Despite uncertainty and stress and challenge, we have found ways to ramp up our joy even now. This energy is sustainable. We can recharge, and preserve and protect our spark, to inspire others. We can share our best energy through our art and innovation. Our gratitude and connection. Our attitude, humor, and words.

In a time of so much unrest, we can respond to the racial injustice, inequality, intolerance, and the other abhorrent behaviors that seek to diminish our humanity, not by diminishing others, but by raising our own energy and leading with our light. By standing up and in together, our energies combined, for something better.

This is our decisive moment, remember?

And the things I used to recharge over the last couple of years, they are keeping my energy high now too.

There is much we can't control. But I can control where to focus my energy. How to share it, to keep the cycle going by doing the things that build or energy, which then restores us again and again.

It's there for you too. This vitality. This chi. The life force. It is sustainable. It's exhilarating. It's meaningful. It's You, Recharged.

What now? What's next?

ACKNOWLEDGMENTS

Our relationships have a significant influence on us.

Thank goodness, because I cannot imagine who I'd be without my friends and family members. These people influence me in all the best ways. I am healthier and happier because of the people I get to love. And very, very grateful.

Thank you and so much love to my family Jerry, Piper, Lynda, and Steve Campbell, Paige Campbell, and Quinn McCarthy. Thanks to the President (and only member) of the Polly Campbell Fan Club, PCFC Ginger Buzzell, and Super Fan Carole Pierce Martins.

Tonya, Sherri, Lori, Megan, Teresa, Regina, Trish, Ingrid, Tracy, Jodi H., Kelly J., Cassandra D., Jodi N., Kelly H., I love you. Thanks for showing up all these years. You've brought the best kind of energy into my life.

Brenda Knight, Associate Publisher of Mango Publishing Group, thanks for coming for me. You are a marvel and I'm honored to work with you. Thanks to Chris McKenney, Robin Miller, Debbie Hartung, Minerve Jean, Hannah Jorstad Paulsen, Geena El-Haj, Yaddyra Peralta, Morena Guerrero, Shawn Hoult, and the entire Mango team. Thrilled to be working with this innovative group.

And thanks to all of you who read and buy books. Books are one way we pass the best energy on.

ABOUT THE AUTHOR

Polly Campbell is the author of four books, including *How to Recharge, How to Live an Awesome Life*, and *Imperfect Spirituality*. She is also the host of the podcast *Polly Campbell, Simply Said: How to Live Well, Do Good, and Be Happy*, and a professional speaker. In addition, Polly writes a blog for *Psychology Today*, and her articles on resilience, psychology, and success strategies appear regularly in other print and online publications. She lives with her husband and daughter in Oregon.

LET'S CONNECT

If you'd like to keep the conversation going, please sign up for my newsletter at www.pollycampbell.com and join my Facebook page at Polly Campbell, Author/Speaker. And listen to the podcast *Polly Campbell, Simply Said* wherever you get your podcasts.

Mango Publishing, established in 2014, publishes an eclectic list of books by diverse authors—both new and established voices—on topics ranging from business, personal growth, women's empowerment, LGBTQ studies, health, and spirituality to history, popular culture, time management, decluttering, lifestyle, mental wellness, aging, and sustainable living. We were recently named 2019 *and* 2020's #1 fastest growing independent publisher by *Publishers Weekly*. Our success is driven by our main goal, which is to publish high quality books that will entertain readers as well as make a positive difference in their lives.

Our readers are our most important resource; we value your input, suggestions, and ideas. We'd love to hear from you—after all, we are publishing books for you!

Please stay in touch with us and follow us at:

Facebook: Mango Publishing
Twitter: @MangoPublishing
Instagram: @MangoPublishing
LinkedIn: Mango Publishing
Pinterest: Mango Publishing
Newsletter: mangopublishinggroup.com/newsletter

Join us on Mango's journey to reinvent publishing, one book at a time.